CROWOOD EQUESTRIAN GUIDES

Basic Jumping

CAROL FOSTER

The Crowood Press

First published in 1991 by
The Crowood Press Ltd
Ramsbury, Marlborough
Wiltshire SN8 2HR

This impression 2001

British Library Cataloguing in Publication Data

Foster, Carol *1952–*
        Basic jumping.
        1. Horse Jumping
        I. Title
        799.25

        ISBN 1–85223–547–0

Disclaimer:
Throughout this book the pronouns 'he', 'him' and 'his' have
been used inclusively and are meant to apply to both males and
females.

Acknowledgements:
Photographs by Louis Milburn.
Line-drawings by Hazel Morgan.

Typeset by Footnote Graphics, Warminster, Wiltshire
Printed by J. W. Arrowsmith Limited, Bristol

CONTENTS · 3

The earliest evidence of horses being domesticated dates from 4,500 years ago with Neolithic cave paintings showing horses kept for milk and flesh. Domesticated mares were eventually used as pack animals for nomadic tribes and from this came the development of the fit animal capable of carrying men for hunting or battle.

Horses became a significant part of Greek civilization from about 2000 BC. First used exclusively for pulling chariots, it was over 1,000 years before the ridden horse came into its own. A race for ridden horses was introduced to the ancient Olympic games in 648 BC, but it is from the Greek cavalry soldier, Xenophon, that we have learned most, not only about Greek horsemanship, but also about the whole development of modern riding.

THE CLASSICAL SCHOOLS

The heavy horses of the Middle Ages which carried the knights of chivalry made way for lighter horses, as weapons and methods of battle changed. High school movements were originally designed as evasive or aggressive tactics in the battlefield and the classical schools of equitation were all cavalry schools. The influence of the first school in Naples spread throughout Europe and notably to Vienna where Spanish horses were imported to found the Spanish Riding School. With a stud established at Lipizza, now in Yugoslavia, these impressive white horses became known as Lipizzaners.

The Spanish School itself lends influence to the French who further developed dressage. Most famous of the French masters in the sixteenth century was de la Guerinère who is known as the father of modern equitation.

THE MODERN SPORTING HORSE

In 1912 equestrian sports were included in the modern Olympic games and the popularity of riding as a leisure sport for all was born. Dressage was popular on the Continent, while British enthusiasm for hunting and riding across country began to find an outlet in show-jumping. However, the Continental riders and course designers were still more adventurous than the

British. They began to construct their 'Derby' courses, with permanent banks, hedges and ditches in their show arenas and linked these with combination fences – doubles and trebles, parallel bars, oxers and 'Jacob's ladders'. The forward style of riding developed by the Italian Frederico Caprilli became essential to tackle the new courses, allowing the horse more freedom of its head and neck, and better use of its back.

In 1948 the Olympic games were held in London and equestrian sports, especially show-jumping, proved popular as spectator sports began to capture public imagination. A year later the three-day event was introduced to Badminton and today, 'eventing', together with show-jumping and dressage, is one of

The traditional British enthusiasm for hunting and riding across country played a fundamental role in the development of show-jumping as a sport.

The popularity of show-jumping grew rapidly after 1948 when the Olympic games were held in London. Televising of big international events from the early 1950s onwards helped to make show-jumping a popular spectator sport as well as encouraging thousands of young riders to take it up for themselves.

the three most popular sports. All these disciplines are popular with younger riders for whom the Pony Club – founded in 1929 and the largest association of riders in the world – provides competition and instruction in most English-speaking countries.

Our natural love of horses, combined with greater exposure of horse sports and greater access to them, enables many thousands of riders world-wide to enjoy riding as a leisure activity. Riding schools provide a basis on which people with no previous knowledge or background of horses can learn and improve their riding even though they may never own a horse. An hour a week may never raise a rider to Olympic standards, but then not all riders seek to compete with others; merely to be close to horses, to form a relationship with a particular horse, and to appreciate the challenge of this is, in itself, sufficient for many.

Are you ready to jump? Really ready? Most young riders cannot wait to shorten their stirrups and take off, but your instructor will want to make sure that you have reached a level of competence before taking this big leap forward.

Safety is always the first consideration where horses and riding are concerned – for your sake, other people's and the pony's. Are you safe?

Competence in all the school paces and correct application of the aids is essential before you can progress to more advanced work. You cannot run before you can walk and you cannot jump before you can walk, trot and canter. Can you apply the aids?

Correct feel for what is happening underneath you is an acquired skill, but one which increasingly you should develop, especially to feel the stride of your pony when approaching fences. Can you *feel* through the seat of your breeches?

Vital Questions to Ask Yourself
Are you
Safe?
Can you apply the
Aids?
Can you
Feel through
the seat of your
breeches?
Do you study
Equitation?
Do you have a
Truly independent
seat?
Can you answer
Yes to all the above?

Competence in your basic school work is necessary before you can progress to more advanced work. Improving your riding on the flat is all part of this.

Equitation sounds very serious but it is the combination of all your skills which makes you into an all-round rider. If you want to go on to jump and improve your skills, you should never stop studying equitation. Do you study equitation?

An independent seat can take years to develop but your instructor will want to see you riding in a way which helps rather than hinders the pony before allowing you to jump. Do you have a truly independent seat?

If your answer is *yes* to all these questions, read on. If not, read on anyway and it will help you in your progress as a rider.

ARE YOU SAFE?

Riding is a risky sport and the faster and higher you go the riskier it becomes. By ensuring you are a competent rider mounted on a pony suited to your level of ability, you can reduce these risks greatly. You may be keen to progress, gallop and jump, but those responsible for you, especially your instructor, must always ensure that your ability matches your ambitions.

If you are riding unaccompanied on a hack, ride sensibly with consideration for others. Never ride out on a horse or pony beyond your capabilities. If you want to jump natural obstacles such as logs or ditches, first make sure that the take-offs and landings are good and are not pot-holed or loose. Make sure that there is no wire in which you might get tangled. Don't tackle large fixed obstacles, however brave you may feel; it is always better to be safe than sorry.

Never ride without correct head and footwear; a jockey skull to British Standard 4472 and proper riding boots in good repair are essential. Gloves help to keep a more secure hold on the reins. Your pony's tack should also be in good repair and his shoes should be renewed well before they reach the smooth and shiny stage.

APPLICATION OF THE AIDS

Your ability as a rider and knowledge of school work also make you safe. Before jumping you should know, and be able to apply, all your aids correctly. You should be able to make your

This young rider has enjoyed a day's hunting but no matter what your mounted activity, always wear correct head and foot gear.

upward and downward transitions and be aware of the rhythm or regularity of footsteps within a pace. With the use of a half-halt, a momentary collection, you should be able to gain your pony's attention before making a different movement or transition. You will need his attention when preparing to jump.

Your leg aid should be effective so that the pony responds to your signal. Your hands must contain the forward energy created by your seat and legs but must remain soft and allowing so that you do not jerk the bit in the pony's mouth, causing pain and maybe making him reluctant to jump.

HOW DO YOU FEEL?

An awareness of what is happening underneath you is a great asset and one which you will acquire increasingly. It is obviously important to be able to tell if the pony is lame or *unlevel* (not taking equal steps). You should also know when you are on the correct canter lead or trot diagonal without looking down to check. Can you make a square halt without checking? Can you tell which leg has been left behind if the halt is not square?

Developing this feel is important for improving your basic riding technique and for jumping. When you become more advanced you will need to assess, and maybe adjust, your pony's stride as you approach a fence. Learning these basics from the beginning so that they become second nature is much easier than having to return to them later.

EQUITATION

A grand-sounding word for riding, but it means rather more than that. It is a lifetime's study, but for the young rider it should mean an understanding of how the horse moves and how to ride the horse forward correctly. Your aim always is to create energy in the pony's quarters by using your legs and seat effectively. This forward movement is combined with *straightness*. The horse should be tracking up and you should have the feeling that you are pushing through from your inside leg to a positive contact in your outside rein. You should build up a strong sense of rhythm and be able to maintain this throughout all paces and transitions. If you ride forward and straight in a regular rhythm, your pony becomes balanced, takes a positive, even contact on the bit, and becomes obedient to your aids.

These are the basics of correct equitation and the well-schooled rider and pony are much more effective and attractive to watch than the unschooled combination.

INDEPENDENT SEAT

The best way to achieve a truly independent seat is by continuing with lunge lessons, even when you have progressed *off* the lunge. Riders at the Spanish Riding School spend their first year having lunge lessons, and top international riders continue to have instruction regularly on the lunge. So, do not think that once you are *off*, that's it. Riding without stirrups and reins helps you mould into the pony and achieve a balanced, deep and relaxed position.

On or off the lunge, do your exercises to keep your neck and upper body free from tension:

1. Shrug your shoulders up to your ears and let them drop down again.
2. Circle your arms alternately. Bring your arm out in front of you with fingers stretched and circle it up, stretching tall as it passes your ear, and sitting deep as your fingers point to your ankle.
3. On the lunge, take both arms straight out to the sides and swivel round from the waist from side to side.
4. On the lunge, take both arms out to the sides and bend forward at the waist, keeping your seat in the saddle and your head up, looking forward.
5. While standing still, circle your head, first dropping your chin down; then bring your ear to your shoulder, head back, ear to other shoulder and chin down again. This may make you feel dizzy so only do it once or twice, starting from left and right.
6. Take your feet out of the stirrups; then, with alternate or

Continue to have lunge lessons to help you achieve a more independent seat.

both legs together, bring your knees right up towards the pommel, then stretch them down and backwards slightly; let them relax in riding position. This helps you sit deep and relaxed and helps you find the correct position.

The importance of the independent seat is that, increasingly, you move more fluently with the horse. All your movement flows with the horse, no matter what he does; nothing you do interferes with the correct action of the pony.

This is vital when jumping to stay and go with the pony to avoid making a bad approach or jabbing him in the mouth when making the jump. If you do ever get left behind when a pony jumps, grab some mane or a neck strap, but at all costs avoid balancing yourself against his mouth.

If you can answer *yes* to all these requirements it is probably time you learned to jump.

If you feel yourself getting left behind, grab some mane or the neck strap to avoid jabbing the pony in the mouth.

rider jabbing horse in mouth

(clamping knee and no lower leg)

A course of jumps is really like a dressage test with obstacles. Jumping is flat work with an extra dimension. It is important that both horse and rider are well schooled in basic equitation to make them more efficient when they jump. The horse should move forward with energy and obedience from the rider's leg aid and he should be straight and balanced to take his fences in good style. The rider should understand how to *save* his horse, always riding with respect for the horse's well-being and not asking of him more than he is capable. The well-schooled horse will be a more successful jumper and less likely to suffer injury than an unschooled one.

For this reason it is important to prepare thoroughly *on the flat* and this is why your early jumping lessons will begin as a progression of flat work. You cannot jump without preparing on the flat, but jumping can be a useful part of improving flat work. You may find that before you have been able to answer *yes* to all the questions in the previous section, your instructor has introduced you to work over ground poles. Arranged in a straight line or around a corner, *trotting* poles, placed 3½–4ft (1.1–1.3m) apart, help the pony to use his hocks actively and to stretch forward with his head and neck. This rounds his back

Your first jumping lesson. Trotting poles help the pony to use his hocks actively, to stretch forward with his head and neck, and strengthen his back muscles.

and strengthens his back muscles which will help him to jump well, as well as improve his performance on the flat. Work over trotting poles will help you become accustomed to jumping position and will help to teach you not to interfere with the pony. For larger ponies and horses, the poles will be placed at 4ft 3in–5ft (1.4–1.7m).

JUMPING POSITION

Your position when jumping is one which helps the pony to use himself over a jump by stretching forward with his head and neck, rounding his back and tucking his legs up underneath him. This is how the horse jumps naturally, and his natural balance and ability are best maintained if the rider transfers his weight forward slightly over the pony's shoulders.

The classical position is modified for jumping. The rider's weight is transferred forward to allow the pony freedom of the back, neck and head. The rider's seat bones should remain close to the saddle to enable him to return quickly to the upright position.

To achieve jumping position you need to shorten your stirrups by two or three holes. This helps you to fold forward from your hips with your upper body and take more weight on your thighs, calves and heels. Your knees should remain bent and your lower leg back and underneath you. Your seat should remain close to the saddle so you can return easily to an upright position and use your seat and back to send your pony forward. This is especially important when tackling combination fences when, after landing from the first element, you need to sit up quickly and ride the horse forward to the next. Do not stand up and bring your body forward out of the saddle or you will lose balance and perhaps send the pony out of balance.

Your hands must be ready to allow the horse freedom of his head and neck. When trotting over poles you can push your hands away from you, allowing the pony more rein. He will then take the rein without the bit catching him in his back teeth.

> **Getting Your Jumping Position Right**
> In conjuction with trotting over poles in jumping position, you can practise on the flat in the school, or out hacking, by trotting and cantering in the forward position. It is important to keep in balance with the pony and to stay with his movement, not be left behind, nor get in front of the action.

TROTTING POLES

The basic exercise involves a line of four to six heavy poles laid on the ground 3½ft–4ft (1.1m–1.3m) apart. The shorter distance is for ponies or shorter-striding horses and the longer one for bigger horses. Longer-striding horses will need a greater distance. At these distances the pony will trot over the poles, simply taking them in his stride. To begin with you may stay in rising trot to negotiate the line of poles, allowing forward with your hands. You may then adopt jumping position and complete the exercise in forward position, but remaining in trot. The pony should take the trotting poles without altering the rhythm of his stride.

WHAT IS A JUMP?

The canter is a modified gallop stride and a jump is taken as a part of a canter or gallop. When you begin to learn to jump, or when the young horse is being trained, the approach is made in trot. This enables you and the pony to keep in better balance and encourages the pony to round his back when jumping.

Three phases of a jump – take-off, suspension and landing – showing how the horse must be allowed freedom to stretch forward with his head and neck.

Because canter is the natural jumping pace, a horse will naturally land in canter, even when he has taken off in trot. It is usual to allow the horse to continue in canter if he does this, and if you have difficulty in obtaining canter this is a good way to make the upward transition.

In the final few strides in his approach to a fence, a horse lowers his head and neck, then raises his head as he picks his forehand up in take-off. The powerful muscles of his quarters help the joints of hips, stifles (equivalent to our knees), and hocks to uncoil like a spring, propelling the horse up and over the fence. When the horse lands, he does so on one foreleg, followed by the other foreleg (the lead leg of canter), and the hind legs.

YOUR FIRST JUMP

A horse being ridden over a fence should be allowed to jump as naturally as he would unmounted. Your job as a rider is, as far as you are able, to allow your pony to do this. Whether or not you have been taking regular lessons – hopefully, you have – you or those teaching you will thoroughly prepare you before starting proper jumping.

A novice rider's first jump is usually introduced at the end of a line of trotting poles. Instead of a line of six poles, the fifth pole is added to the sixth to make a small fence. This can be either a cross pole or a single rail with the other pole used as a *filler*. This first little jump will be no higher than 1½–2ft

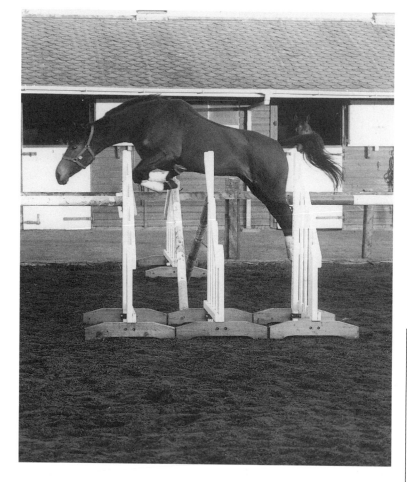

A horse jumping loose, in good style. A horse being ridden over a fence should be allowed to jump as naturally as he would unmounted.

(0.5–0.7m) and should be ridden as though it were just another pole. Ride straight forward with confidence and the pony will pop over with ease.

Don't get over-anxious about the jump. Remember, your pony has four legs and powerful hindquarters. He does not have to use speed to clear the jump. He is capable of jumping bigger fences from a standstill. You do not have to ride fast into the fence, but you must have energy. You should remain in rising or sitting trot, keeping the upper body either upright or slightly forward, with your seat in the saddle. This way you can ride forward with energy and keep your seat should your pony decide to stop or dodge out.

What is a Good Jump?

1. The horse makes a calm, steady, straight approach.
2. He takes off as though from a small platform.
3. He jumps over the fence with his front legs tucked well up underneath him.
4. He flexes the joints in his hind legs and keeps them as close as possible to his body.
5. He stretches forward with his head and neck and appears to lift and round his back (bascule).
6. He lands lightly and continues calmly and straight.

A rider makes a good approach by riding an accurate turn towards the pole, looking up towards a landmark beyond the exercise.

Always look up and straight ahead. As you make your approach to the poles and fence, fix your eyes on a landmark in front of you and keep looking at it. As the pony takes off over the jump, push your hands away from you to make sure he has plenty of rein. Fold forward a little more from the hips and allow him to round his back. As he lands, sit up and ride straight forward again.

Everyone has a few butterflies when they start to jump – even sometimes when they've been jumping a long time – but if you can ride every step positively your pony will do the rest for you.

In all your riding you should always think about riding the horse forward and straight. A horse which is not obedient to your *forward* aids – your back, seat and legs – will not have sufficient energy to jump. The hindquarters are the horse's engine compartment, but if you take your foot off the accelerator, that is stop *driving* him forward, the horse will stop.

He must also be straight, both in his school work and on the approach to fences. He should work on one track, his hind feet falling into the prints left by his forefeet, and you should have a feeling of equal weight on the rein to each hand. On a circle or corner, the horse's spine should be uniformly curved around the line of the circle. If the horse is not forward he cannot truly be straight. He might make it over one fence but as you start to ask him more demanding questions he will answer by refusing or running out.

WHAT IS GYMNASTIC JUMPING?

To improve rhythm, suppleness, strength, obedience and the ability to lengthen or shorten his stride, the horse is schooled over *grids* – lines of poles and small fences set at distances varying from no stride to two non-jumping strides between the fences. When you are learning to jump, your pony will probably be well-schooled in such exercises and will help you to improve your own suppleness, application of the aids and ability to ride him forward and straight. When the pony is going freely and calmly, you will find it easier to sit correctly. Without worrying about the horse, you can relax and concentrate on your own balance and sense of stride.

Gridwork is hard work for horses and ponies. If you are schooling on your own you should not spend too much time in any one session on grids, even though it is good fun for the rider. The distances between the poles and small fences are especially worked out by your instructor to be suitable for the ponies or horses in a class. It is important, especially with young, inexperienced horses, to be precise with distances, as wrong distances could cause a horse to arrive badly at a fence, encouraging him to stop. Horses and ponies remember bad experiences.

During these early stages, it is useful for you to try to develop a feel for the strides your pony is taking. However, it is

A young rider negotiates a simple gymnastic exercise. The distances are set to allow the pony to jump easily within his stride and the rider can relax and concentrate on her own position and sense of stride.

a mistake early on to become so absorbed with strides that you start to interfere with the forward movement of the pony. As a novice, you should try to sit as still and quietly as you can, concentrating only on staying with your pony. This will give you quite enough to think about, without trying to *place* your pony before a fence. The distances between poles and fences will allow the pony to arrive *right* at the fences and he will take them in his stride.

THE RIDER'S POSITION

As more jumps are introduced, it becomes even more important for you to be in the right position. This is one which allows the horse freedom in his back over the fence but which is never too far from the upright *safety* position in the saddle. As you practise you will become more flexible in your upper body and this is essential when one or more fences are added to the jumping grid.

If you stand in the stirrups or position yourself too far forward you weaken your position, so:

This rider has lost her safety position. She has lost contact with the saddle and her leg has come much too far back. She is not in a position to be able to pick up the reins quickly on landing and ride the horse forward to the next fence.

1. Your lower leg slips back and does not maintain impulsion.
2. The horse may stop or run out and you are more likely to fall off.
3. You lose positive contact with the horse's mouth (your hands tend to slip forward) and therefore control; the horse is more likely to stop or run out. An excitable horse, on the other hand, will take it as a signal to rush his fences.

The rider's position when jumping is not fixed. As the pony takes off you should:

1. Bend in the middle, from your hips, so your upper body is positioned over the pony's shoulders.
2. Allow forward with your hands, so he can stretch his head and neck.
3. Keep looking up and forward.
4. Keep the lower leg still and close to the pony's sides.

Now you can begin to see the value of establishing a good independent seat, for you must have the control over your own body to allow flexibility of your position.

Landing from the first of a grid or course of fences becomes

take-off

position over fence

landing

The rider's position over a fence.

especially important. If you collapse on landing, your pony will stop and you will not have enough energy to jump the next fence.

RIDING THROUGH A GRID

As in all your riding, you should continue to ride forward and straight in rhythm and balance. As in trotting poles, the approach is the time you have to make the greatest effect on the jumps your pony makes. In making your approach you should remember the following:

1. Look round towards the grid before making your turn.
2. Make a good turn down towards the grid, using the turn to push the horse into your outside hand with the inside leg.
3. Look towards your landmark.
4. Keep the pony forward and straight in regular rhythm.
5. Do not interfere with the pony when jumping, or try to influence his stride.
6. Keep riding straight and forward after each fence.

Although you should make your approach in trot, on landing from the first fence the pony will probably canter – the natural

Your Position on Landing
1. Bring the upper body back into an upright position.
2. Be ready to shorten the reins again so you have contact with the pony's mouth, and keep him straight.
3. Keep the lower leg back and underneath you, bending your leg at the knee, close to the pony's side, in order to push him forward.
4. Keep looking towards the next fence or towards your landmark. Don't let the pony dodge to one side on landing.

jumping pace. If the pony offers canter, allow him to continue in this pace, rather than trying to return to trot. If you were riding a pony which tended to rush and flatten over his fences, gridwork may not be a suitable exercise as it may tend to make him more excitable. The aim of the exercise is that, by maintaining impulsion and rhythm, the horse will round his topline and strengthen his back muscles.

PLACING POLES

To help you further when starting to jump, your instructor may use a single pole placed on the ground 8½–9½ft (2.6–3m) in front of a fence. You should ignore this and simply ride for the fence with your eye fixed on your landmark. A placing pole encourages the pony to organize his stride and arrive correctly at the fence for take-off.

Gridwork is not always a suitable exercise for excitable ponies. They tend to rush and flatten over the fences.

BUILDING UP GRIDWORK

A basic grid will probably consist of four trotting poles followed

by a small fence, a placing pole and another small fence. The fences themselves will be small – even for horses and experienced riders, the fences in a grid should not exceed 3ft (0.9m). It is not important to teach the horse to jump high fences; if his gymnastic or athletic ability is improved, as well as his obedience, you can safely leave the higher fences to the competition ring. The spreads of your first fences will be not greater than 3–3ft 3in (0.9–1m).

Smaller ponies may need shorter distances and big horses will need greater distances. This is why it is important to have professional help.

When you are able to ride well through the basic exercises your instructor will start to make the grids slightly more demanding. The fences will remain small but they will be more varied and include small spreads. Your pony may have room for two non-jumping strides or only one stride between fences. This means he will land and take one or two strides before taking off again. As a very gymnastic exercise, in which you have to ride every inch of the way, your instructor may set the fences at *bounce* distance, which means there is no room for a non-jumping stride and the pony has to take off as soon as his hind feet land. If you know what hard work it is to double skip, you can imagine what is involved for the pony. You must be able to keep the pony like a spring between your hand and leg so that all his energy is channelled into popping neatly through the grid.

Approximate Distances for Gridwork
No stride between a trotting pole and a small fence: 8½ft (2.6m).
No stride between two small fences: 9½ft (3m).
One stride between two small fences: 18ft (5.6m).
Two strides between two small fences: 33ft (10m).

Distances for a simple grid of placing poles and fences.

Insert diagonal pole on each fence in alternate directions to keep horse straight.

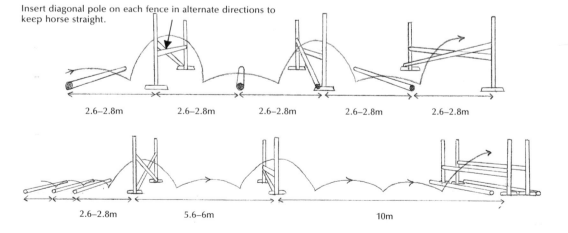

| 2.6–2.8m | 2.6–2.8m | 2.6–2.8m | 2.6–2.8m | 2.6–2.8m |

| 2.6–2.8m | 5.6–6m | 10m |

If you have spent time educating your 'seat' to develop a feel for what is happening underneath you, you will be acquiring skills as a sensitive and effective rider.

GETTING THE FEEL OF NON-JUMPING STRIDES

From the earliest days on the lunge you should have learnt to recognize the footfalls in each pace and know where the horse's legs are at any time in a phase of a stride.

You should have a feel for the rhythm of a pace and be jumping through small grids fluently. As you ride through these, test yourself and count the number of strides your pony takes between landing and take-off. It is a good exercise to count out loud and your instructor can tell how accurate your feel is.

For early basic jumping you need not worry nor attempt to lengthen or shorten the stride, nor try to tell the pony where to take off. The construction of the grid will take care of these things. Your job is to ride fluently forward, keeping the pony straight, but your developing feel will be a useful asset later.

Sequence of steps through double combination showing one non-jumping stride.

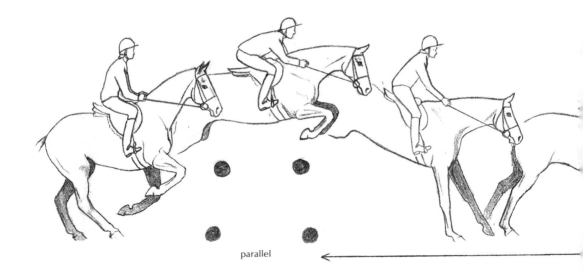

parallel

RELATED DISTANCES

Depending upon the size and stride of the pony you are riding, you may find that two long strides for one horse becomes three short strides for another. The distances also vary with the type, height and spread of the obstacles involved. On televised show-jumping commentaries you may have heard the commentators speak about related distances. This means the distance between one fence in relation to another. The distance between two upright fences needs to be slightly greater than that between two parallels because of the horse's line over the fence. Distances also need to be varied according to the terrain on which the course is built (up or downhill), the ground conditions (heavy or hard) and whether the course is indoors or out. Generally, indoor distances are shorter than out.

The variation in distances is really quite small, but it is very important to have it right. Especially in the early stages when you are developing a feel for jumping, your instructor has to use his experience of a particular pony and his powers of observation to set the correct distances.

If you are building your own grids and combinations it is important to get it right or you might give both you and your

m ————————————————————————→ upright

A horse and a pony tackle the same fence. Note how the pony stretches over the fence, of which the horse appears to make little, indicating the different striding.

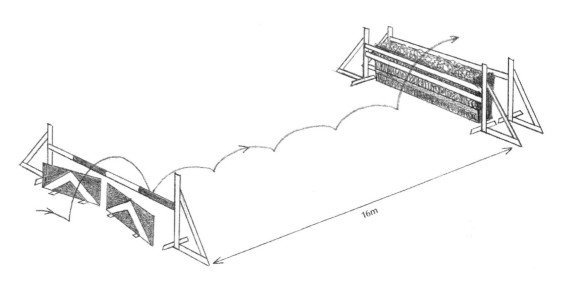

pony's confidence a knock. Fences should not exceed 3ft (0.9m) and your distances should range: 18ft (5.6m) for one stride and 33ft (10m) for two strides between two small uprights; 20–21ft (6–6.5m) for one stride and 34ft (10.5m) for two strides as spreads are introduced.

Experienced riders and trainers vary distances between fences to encourage their horses to take longer or shorter strides, but the novice should not attempt this unless under instruction.

4-stride related distance.

STYLES OF FENCE

As you become more competent, your instructor will introduce different styles of fence into the combinations and grids. While you are learning, it is important for your confidence that your pony tackles all kinds of fences willingly. The more confident a feel the pony gives you, the happier you will feel about pushing him on towards his fences. These will not necessarily be higher, but they may pose a problem for you as a rider. Your pony may find more brightly coloured or unusual fences 'spooky' and will need to be ridden forward more positively.

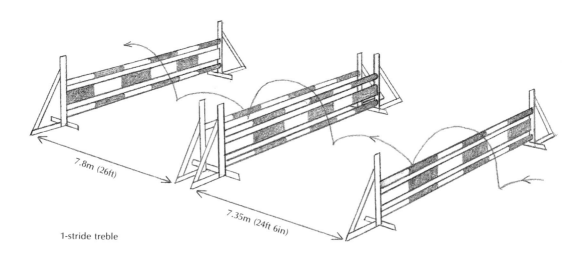

7.8m (26ft)

7.35m (24ft 6in)

1-stride treble

A treble combination of upright/parallel/upright with one non-jumping stride between each element.

COMBINATION FENCES

These may consist of two or three parts, a double or a treble, which will be built at distances closely related to the types of fence they are. These distances will give your pony room to make one, two or three non-jumping strides between the elements of the combination.

The basic types of obstacles which will be met, either as single fences or as parts of a combination, are: upright, parallel (square oxer), staircase (ascending oxer) and pyramid. In big international show-jumping you will see that course builders go to town in designing all kinds of unique and attractive fences, but they still conform to the basic types.

Watch how the horses tackle the various fences. At big, wide, ascending fences, the take-off has to be closer to the base of the fence than for upright fences or the horse will not make the spread. On the other hand, if he gets too close to an upright he will not make the height. Fences are related to one another at a distance of up to 80ft (20m) and with big show jumps a matter of inches can be critical and make the rider's task a tricky one.

For novice riders, the use of a placing pole 8½–9½ft (2.6–3m) in front of a fence helps to remove the guesswork and puts the horse right for take-off. It is easy to get over-anxious, but until you are very experienced you should always wait for the pony to take off and then go with him. A placing pole helps you to

triple bar

narrow gate

parallel

wall

upright

pyramid

The various types of fence you may meet in the competition ring.

do this. You should not try to interfere with or place your pony until you are much more experienced. Course builders at an advanced level site their fences at angles and distances to make the riders really think. Although it is interesting for the novice to appreciate how much difference a matter of inches can make, it is not a subject which you will have to deal with for a long time. For novices, a course builder's aim is to encourage horse and rider, and distance problems should not be introduced. If you are building a grid or course yourself, always make the distances easy for your pony.

If you are practising on your own, always make sure your fences have a good ground line to enable your pony to make a good jump over the fence. If there is no ground line, or a false line on unlevel ground, it is more difficult for your pony to take off correctly. Young horses, particularly, tend to be put off by fences which show a lot of daylight, so if you should be riding an inexperienced pony always make the fences as inviting as possible. Confidence is a two-way process between horse and rider. Never overface your pony or yourself.

Gridwork will help you maintain a good position while riding positively forward and help you to get a feeling for the jumping and non-jumping strides of your pony. It will teach you to approach your fences straight and to ride your pony straight and forward throughout the line of poles and jumps and when you come out of the exercise. When you can trot and canter through these exercises, it is time to start putting together individual fences to make small, straightforward courses.

A DRESSAGE TEST WITH JUMPS

When you start to ride a course of fences you will find how important it is to ride accurately. You will also begin to learn how this is more easily achieved on a well-schooled horse with a well-educated rider. A course of jumps should be tackled as precisely and fluently as though you were riding a dressage test, remembering all the basics of good riding. Ninety per cent of jumping is in the track taken around the course and the approach to the fence. If you present your pony at his fences correctly you cannot do more. Once he has left the ground you can but sit still and keep looking ahead.

The Jumping Track
Your *track* around a course of jumps is the path you travel around the whole course – your approaches, jumps and landings. In order to ride a good track you should first know what fences you have to jump and in what order. You must keep your pony balanced and attentive and not have to make last-minute decisions about where you are going. Cutting corners will not give your pony the best opportunity to clear his fences.

A course of jumps should be ridden as accurately as a dressage test.

Once your pony has left the ground there is nothing you can do but sit still and look ahead, as this workmanlike pair.

MAKING GOOD TURNS

In riding a good track it is essential that you make an accurate turn into your straight approach. You can only do this if you have an eye on the fence before making the turn. All too often you see riders looking down at their hands or the horse's neck. You should know what these look like without checking! Always look up at where you are going. It will seem as though the pony follows your eye almost automatically.

In all your riding, a turn is a good opportunity to check that you have plenty of energy coming forward from the pony's quarters. By looking up, sitting really tall, and making a series of half-halts, slight checks with the outside rein, then pushing on again with the inside leg, you gain the pony's attention and balance him prior to making your approach. The energy you

Do not attempt to cut corners and ride fences at an angle. Always ride straight, sit straight and look up at where you are going.

create is contained in the hands until you release the energy, like a spring, over the jump.

Starting with single fences, more will be added until you can ride them together as a course. Your instructor may use a placing pole initially to help your pony take off accurately. You should keep looking up and ride for the fence, not the placing pole. Over the fence you should already be looking towards the next fence and on landing you should always be ready to pick the pony up and ride forward.

BALANCING AND CHANGING REIN

To begin with, it is probably better to continue to approach your first fence in trot. This helps your pony to make a better jump. He will land in canter and, providing you can maintain a good, active, bouncy canter, you may remain in this pace for the rest of the course.

It helps you if the first courses that you tackle are kept all on the same rein. This means that the canter lead is the same all the way round. If the fences are arranged basically in a right-handed circle you should stay on right canter lead; if on the left rein, the left or near foreleg will be the leading leg.

Your ability to feel what is happening underneath you becomes important again. Just because your course of fences

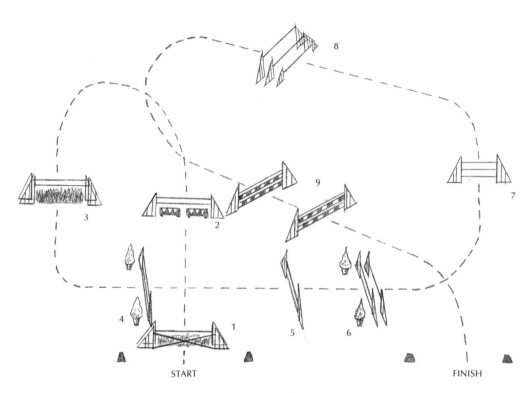

START   FINISH

A course arranged on the left rein. (1) rustic cross rail and brush filler (2) upright with filler (3) parallel with brush (4) upright planks (5) upright rails 2 strides (6) into parallel rails (7) narrow stile (8) triple bar (9) 1-stride double.

is arranged on the right rein, your pony will not automatically land with his right leg leading. Rather than continuing the course in counter-canter (left leg leading on the right rein) you should come back to trot and rebalance your pony. You may then ask for right canter, or remain in a balanced, active trot to approach the next fence. If you have difficulty in achieving canter it is better to stay in trot, otherwise you may succeed only in pushing the pony into a fast, unbalanced trot and miss the next fence entirely. Do not be in too much of a rush or panic about riding a course. Take your time, especially to keep your pony balanced.

You can help to make sure that your pony does land on the correct lead by looking towards your next fence. If you are looking in the direction you want to travel, it is very likely that your pony will take up the correct canter lead automatically. If your next fence is straight ahead, it doesn't matter which leg your pony lands on, but it is a good exercise for you to be able to feel which it is without looking down.

A young rider and pony make a nicely balanced jump. By looking up in the direction you want to travel you will help your pony to take up the correct canter lead.

A course designed with one change of rein.

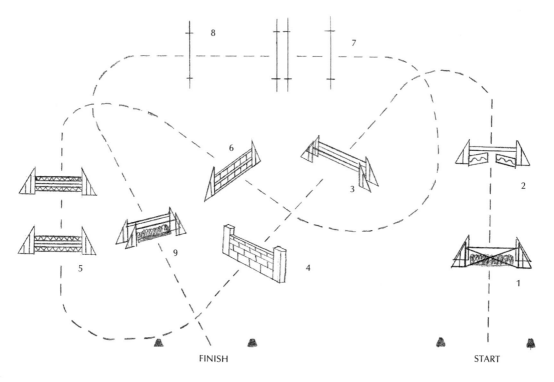

When you can ride accurately around a course with no change of direction, it is time to have a change of rein, probably with the fences arranged in a figure of eight. To make a simple change of rein in canter on the flat, bring your pony back to trot, rebalance, change the canter aid and ask for your new canter lead. Use your half-halts and make sure you have a positive feel in your outside hand. You should always feel that the pony is taking you forward, especially when jumping. If your figure-of-eight course has a fence in the centre on the diagonal, your pony will probably change legs over the fence if you are looking where you are going.

KEEPING A GOOD POSITION

When novice riders become anxious about jumping, they tend to lean forward. This weakens the seat and the lower leg comes back, giving you less control over the pony. When the upper body comes forward, the reins usually go slack and there is then no contact with the pony's mouth. The pony then gives up on the rider. If he is a dull type he will run out of steam and stop at the first opportunity. If he is nervous or excitable he will lack confidence in you and rush at the fences.

Keep a good upright position around the course with your seat always ready to push forward. Stay in the driving seat until

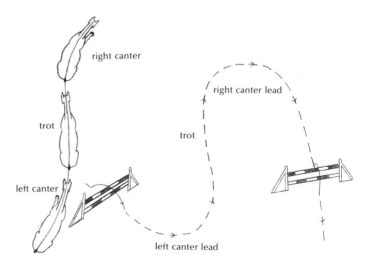

right canter

right canter lead

trot

trot

left canter

left canter lead

The stages of a simple change of leg through trot.

the pony takes off. Always wait for the pony; don't get over-anxious and throw the reins at him three strides away from the fence. You will only ride him into the bottom of the fence.

TACKLING COMBINATION FENCES

As your courses become a little more complicated, your instructor will introduce double and treble combination fences. Your earlier lessons through grids must be remembered here. You must have lots of energy in reserve to allow your pony to spring over the two or three fences. He should have his head up and his eye on the fence. You should be looking at a point beyond the last fence. If you are looking at the first fence and your pony is on a long rein and lazy stride, you may end up in the bottom of that fence.

> **Approximate Distances Between Combination Elements**
> One stride: 18–20ft (5.6–6m)
> Two strides: 31–33ft (9.5–10m)
> Three strides: 45–46ft (14–14.5m)

Always keep your leg aid on and maintain an active, bouncy stride. You should be able to ask the pony to lengthen or shorten his stride on the flat so that you can either send him on or collect him up, generating plenty of power to enable him to make good jumps. Between the elements of a combination be ready to pick up the reins again quickly on landing, sit tall and balance the pony for the next part. Keep him straight so that he cannot duck out.

If you are making your own course of jumps, neither the height nor the width between the elements of a combination should exceed 3ft (0.9m) – this is plenty to practise over. It is always useful to have a friend, preferably a knowledgeable one, on the ground to help you to assess how your pony is coping with the distances you have set. He or she can help adjust the fences if necessary and, of course, put back those which are knocked down.

A given distance for one pony may be more difficult for another and will always depend on the ground conditions or whether the ground is level or slopes either uphill or downhill. Experienced help is essential to enable you to appreciate the technical problems.

Professionally-made show jumps are wonderful things to have, but they are very expensive. It is much better fun to use your own imagination and, with the help of an experienced person, design and make your own.

RAW MATERIALS

Everyone is being encouraged to recycle nowadays, so look around your house, yard or garden to see what old, unused items may be recycled into practice jumps. If you have had alterations made in your house there should be plenty of old material around which would make good fillers for fences:

1. Old doors (hinges and handles removed) can be painted brightly and used to fill upright fences. Alternatively, they could be propped against a pole at an angle to make a slight spread. You could paint them like a wall!
2. Baths (taps removed and edges checked for sharpness) can be filled with soil and planted with flowers for an eye-catching filler. You would have to do this one in a permanent position as it would be too heavy to move around.
3. Paint pots (handles removed) can be painted brightly and lined up to make a ground line or filler. Make them stable by filling them with water or sand and replacing their lids.
4. An old table – perhaps with the legs cut shorter – would make a good *table* fence. This would be quite narrow so you would have to have a stile-type of fence.

A group of young riders get busy constructing a fence with upturned buckets.

In the garden or garage you may have:

1. Car tyres. These are very good as fillers, or, if you have enough, can be stacked to make stands.
2. Oil drums. If you can get hold of the 40-gallon drums these make excellent stands on their sides or ends. A row of drums on their sides makes a good fence. Smaller oil drums make good ground lines when arranged in a row on their sides or fillers on their ends. Check that the drums have not contained poisonous or caustic materials. Check with the owner first before handling them.
3. Brushwood (from hedge or tree pruning). Tie this in bundles for filling fences.
4. Logs. While these may eventually be necessary for a log fire in your fireplace, they can be used to build an interesting log pile fence. Let someone show you how to stack the logs so that they are secure and will not tumble down easily.
5. Fallen branches. If the wind has brought down any tree branches, particularly conifers, you may be able to use these as fillers for wings until the greenery dies off. If you have room and can get hold of fallen tree trunks, you can have these arranged at distances of about 10ft (3m) as a grid to canter through.
6. Trees. If you have the space you could be environmentally friendly and start your own permanent Derby course by planting some evergreen trees in a row of about 10–12ft (3–4m). If you plant something like *Cupressus leylandii*, these will eventually bush out and you can trim the tops to make an impressive hedge.
7. Straw bales make a good filler or a solid fence on their own. Stood on end they also make good stands or can be used as wings if the pony tends to run out.

Making Your Own Jump
1. Fallen trees, if not too big, make a good natural jump with a spread.
2. Post and rail fences are more versatile if their top rail is removable, allowing you to jump in and out of the field.
3. A ditch could be jumped before a small fence (don't forget to put a ground line on the take-off side) or as a middle *filler* of a double-bar fence. If it is fairly wide you could place a pole over the top to make a trakehner. If your ditch is filled with water, or if you have a stream you can splash through, this provides an excellent practice for cross country. Make sure your approach and entry into the water are as inviting as possible, and that the stream bed is not boggy or slippery.

NATURAL SURROUNDINGS

Look around the area you have available for making jumps and see what the natural terrain offers. Perhaps you have a bank or a ditch which you can negotiate just as it is; otherwise, you can build a fence around it. Depending upon the steepness of the bank, you could have a small fence at the top to make a drop

Fallen trees make good natural jumps. Make sure take-offs and landings are safe.

Straw bales are very versatile in fence building.

fence, or you could have a ski jump with a fence at the bottom. Don't be too ambitious – keep the fences small.

STANDS AND POLES

Stands are the most difficult to improvise as the uprights must be sturdy and safe, allowing the pole to be dislodged easily. The poles should be solid and quite heavy. Flimsy sticks are not so easily seen by the horse and may cause accidents.

Stands are fairly easy to make with the help of another capable person and the right materials. A piece of wood measuring 4sq in (10sq cm) and 3½–4ft (1.1–1.3m) high can be fixed to a broad base of four feet, each measuring 4 × 2 × 24in (10cm × 5cm × 60cm), and each one nailed to each side of the stand. Holes for jump cups can be drilled or pegs inserted at a slight upward angle to hold the pole in position. The finished article should be solid, heavy and stand firm. There should be no sharp edges or protruding screws or nails.

More versatile than stands, and easier to make, are jumping blocks, with a shallow dip made in one side so that the pole does not roll out. These could be made from prepared wood or logs but they need to be of uniform size if you are going to stack them. A proprietary make of plastic jumping block is available, and six of these would help you to get started.

If you live near Forestry Commission land, you should be able to get hold of poles quite easily and at no great cost. These are usually available in lengths of 10–12ft (3.1–3.6m), with or without the bark removed. It is useful if the ends have been rounded, smaller twigs and branches removed and the stumps smoothed down. If you want to paint the poles, those with the bark removed are better. Half-length poles are good for making a narrow stile fence.

Sleepers or telegraph poles make good ground poles for a grid lane or solid fillers for cross-country fences.

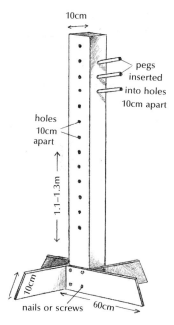

Construction of a simple jump stand.

SAFETY FIRST

In all your DIY efforts, think very carefully about what you are creating. Will it be safe for your pony to jump? Remember to keep to the following guidelines:

1. Make fences which he can see easily.
2. Always have a good ground line from which to take off.
3. Check that there are no sharp edges.
4. Make sure poles will be dislodged.
5. Keep all your jumps in good repair.
6. Keep all your take-offs and landings smooth – vary the positions of your fences (except permanent ones).
7. Make sure all your tack is in good repair and that you have tightened your girth before jumping.
8. Make your jumping fun.
9. *Do not* make anything in which your pony might catch his feet or tangle his legs.
10. *Do not* leave protruding nails or screws.
11. *Do not* ask your pony to jump from very boggy ground or rock-hard ground.
12. *Do not* ride a pony which is beyond your capabilities, for example either a novice pony or a strong, excitable one.

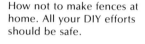

How not to make fences at home. All your DIY efforts should be safe.

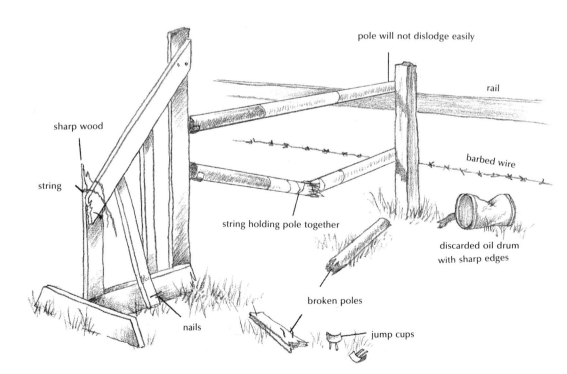

pole will not dislodge easily

rail

sharp wood

barbed wire

string

string holding pole together

discarded oil drum with sharp edges

nails

broken poles

jump cups

13. *Do not* leave jump cups in stands which aren't being used; tidy them away safely.
14. *Do not* over-exert your pony or yourself by building fences which are too big.

As long as you keep to the safety guidelines, you can make your fences as 'spooky' as you like. When you take your pony to competitions there will be different types of fence. If he is used to meeting unusual obstacles at home it will make it less difficult for him when he is out – added to which you will both be more confident in your abilities to jump the less usual fences.

PROFESSIONALLY-MADE JUMPS

It is great if you can have some professionally-made jumps. You might manage to obtain some from an auction or some-times old BSJA fences are advertised for sale. Even if you have only two or three sets of wings, it helps you to vary your DIY efforts. A set of planks is useful and a gate provides something a little different. Also, if you only have home-made stands, you will need to buy jump cups but, bit by bit, you should be able to assemble a really good and interesting 'course'.

Look after your jumps and, if possible, store them away in a shed during the winter to preserve the wood. Painting the poles and fillers annually is a good idea and with a few friends to do it together you can have a really artistic time!

Preserve your show jumps with an annual painting.

We tend to talk about *dressage* and *jumping* as though they were separate sports. True, some riders prefer one to the other, and some horses are more suited to one rather than the other, but work in the school should be a balance of the two. Dressage gives horse and rider balance and coordination to jump; jumping gives excitement and flair to flat work. Any schooling session can be enhanced by some pole work, providing your pony does not tend to be too excited by jumping.

WARMING-UP EXERCISES

Before jumping you should always prepare correctly on the flat. You need to warm up your horse's muscles before he starts more strenuous work, so spend ten minutes or so going through basic school movements. Spend two or three minutes in walk, first on a long rein, then picking up the rein and asking for an active pace. Make some turns and circles, some quarter- and half-pirouettes (turning the forehand about the quarters) and some half-circles returning to the track to change the rein. Work equally on both reins.

Move forward to trot, going large, then making 66ft (20m)

Leg yielding is a good straightening exercise in which the horse should move forward and slightly sideways from your inside leg to a positive contact in your outside hand.

After work your pony can be encouraged to take the rein forward and down, stretching his head and neck while maintaining an active walk.

circles. Ride changes of rein across the diagonal of the school, not forgetting to change your diagonal; you should sit as the outside shoulder comes back. Ride good turns, pushing the pony well into his corners with your inside leg, and make accurate, round circles (*not* egg shapes). Use your half-halt to balance your pony and store up extra energy. Ask your pony for some lengthened strides when coming out of a corner down the long side of the school. Check that he is attentive and forward to your leg aid.

Do some work on both reins in canter; get up off the pony's back and canter cross-country style a couple of times around the school on each rein. Make your changes of rein by a simple change of leg through walk across the centre of the school. When you feel your pony is working well and is attentive to you, responding readily to your aids, return to walk and allow him a little breather while allowing out the rein. If he has been working properly he will take the rein and stretch his neck forward and down.

Your pony quickly should stop breathing more rapidly from the canter and, unless the weather is very hot and humid, should not be sweating. If laboured breathing or sweating continues, your pony may not be fit enough for the work you are doing or he may be ill. Check with someone more knowledgeable before continuing. One of the most serious prob-

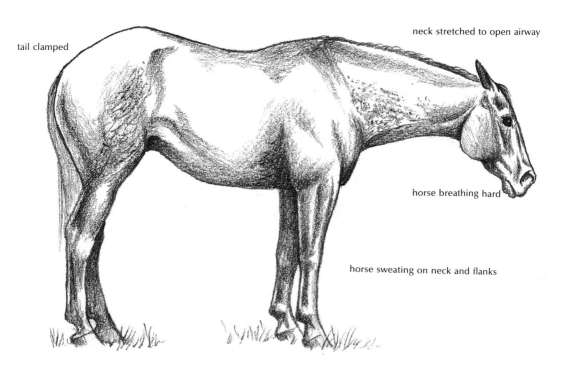

neck stretched to open airway

tail clamped

horse breathing hard

horse sweating on neck and flanks

Do not risk over-exercising an unfit horse. Signs of mismanagement can be very distressing and, at worst, potentially fatal for a horse.

lems associated with working too hard on an unfit horse is an illness called azoturia. This is a type of cramp which affects the pony's quarters and is caused by a toxic substance released from the pony's unfit muscles. The affected pony will be in pain and refuse to move. You should keep his back warm and get professional help immediately.

WHAT TO JUMP

Start with some straightforward gridwork to encourage the pony to use himself athletically. Approach in trot but allow him to continue in canter. Arranging the poles around part of the perimeter of a circle encourages the pony to stretch forward, round his back and engage his hocks; a good exercise to improve his flat work.

If you are under instruction, or have an experienced helper, the distances and obstacles in your grid can be altered, offering you different challenges. Whatever task is set, keep your pony forward and straight, riding forward positively all

the time. A good exercise to make sure you can keep your pony *straight* on a circle is to have two fences placed on each side of a circle. You will need to present your pony at his fences straight, while still keeping him on a continual turn. You will have a very positive feel on your outside rein as your inside leg pushes *through* to keep the pony out on the circle.

After jumping these individual fences, you may go once or twice around a course, perhaps taking each fence individually first before putting it together.

Remember all your basic flat-work lessons when riding your track; ride the course like a dressage test over fences. If you have any kind of problem with your jumping it could be that you have prepared incorrectly on the flat, so you must go back to basics.

Arranging poles around the perimeter of a circle encourages the pony to step forward, round his back and engage his hocks.

LENGTH OF SESSION

Don't spend any longer than about twenty minutes actually jumping, and don't ride repeatedly through a grid; four to six times will be enough as it is very hard work for the horse.

Schooling fences need not be big, whatever your level of experience. The largest the novice need consider is 3ft (0.9m) height and 3ft (0.9m) spread and, surprisingly, this need not be much greater for the experienced rider. Gymnastic jumping improves the handiness and obedience of the horse, giving him the athletic ability and obedience to clear higher fences in the competition ring.

The time to finish a jumping session is when the horse and rider have made some good jumps. The experienced combination may only jump once or twice then go for a good, reward-

Gymnastic jumping improves the handiness and obedience of the horse.

ing and refreshing hack. If your jumping sessions are not under instruction, do not tire your pony, jumping time and time again; however much fun you may find it, your pony's legs will become tired and he will become bored – a recipe for trouble.

NOVICE RIDERS AND NOVICE HORSES

Until you are more experienced, do not be tempted to ride novice horses. This is a job for experienced trainers. You would not expect to be taught by someone who knows no more than yourself; you would learn nothing, get confused and give up. It is no different for horses. A willing, experienced pony, however, can be a teacher to you, boosting your confidence and giving you a good feel for jumping.

If you have your own pony, don't spend too much time on your own. Take him to a school for a lesson about once a month at least. This will prevent you from continuing to make the same mistakes, as well as get you used to jumping away from home – very important preparation for competitions.

Warming Down
Do not, after making your final jump, simply put the pony away. Letting his muscles relax again gradually after work is as important as warming him up before work. Without this he will stiffen up and be sore the next day, making him reluctant to work. Spend ten minutes warming down in the school, trotting and walking on an increasingly long rein, allowing the pony to take his nose right down to the ground if he wants to. Alternatively, you could allow him to relax by going out for a gentle, short hack and give him a change of scenery.

The majority of ponies you ride, particularly in a riding school will be fitted with straightforward snaffle bridles. The snaffle bit has many different variations but any bit which basically consists of a mouthpiece and rings (sometimes with cheek pieces) falls into the category of a snaffle. Correctly schooled ponies respond to the action of a snaffle and there should be no need, unless the pony is a show pony, to ride him in anything else.

THE ACTION OF THE BIT

A bit works by placing pressure on the pony's tongue and sensitive toothless edge (or bars) of his mouth. The pony responds to this pressure by relaxing his jaw and moving forward into a positive, constant contact with the bit and therefore the rider's hands.

Things go wrong when a rider fails to reward the pony's obedience by allowing him to take this contact. The action of a rider's hands should be one which continually *plays a tune* with the horse's mouth. Allowing, but not giving away, and,

Position of a snaffle bit in the pony's mouth as it lies on the tongue and bars.

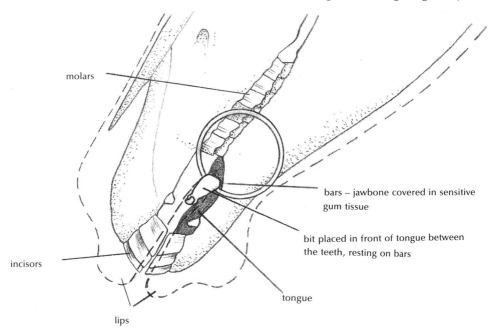

molars

bars – jawbone covered in sensitive gum tissue

bit placed in front of tongue between the teeth, resting on bars

incisors

tongue

lips

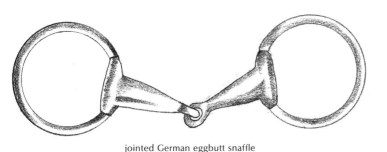

Two variations of the snaffle – the jointed German eggbutt and the vulcanized straight bar.

jointed German eggbutt snaffle

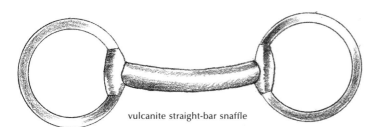

vulcanite straight-bar snaffle

together with the combination of back, seat and legs, momentarily restraining to keep the pony in balance and rhythm.

Hands which become hard and dead – usually associated with fixed wrists and forearms – can ruin a pony's mouth. This is usually done with a young pony who lacks balance and training and is one of the reasons why the training of young horses should be left to sympathetic professionals.

Once a pony has found the action of the bit painful, he will try to evade it, perhaps by throwing his head, getting his tongue over the bit or swallowing his tongue. Injury to the tongue or bars of a pony's mouth can ruin their sensitivity and create a hard mouth which pulls and leans on the bit. Pain in the mouth may cause the pony to bolt uncontrollably and, unfortunately, rather than returning to basics, the impatient human reaction is to fit harsher bits and back them up with all kinds of other artificial aids.

THE PELHAM BIT

The pelham bit, again in many variations, is a combination of the two bits of a double bridle. It works by exerting leverage

The pelham and a variation, the kimblewick.

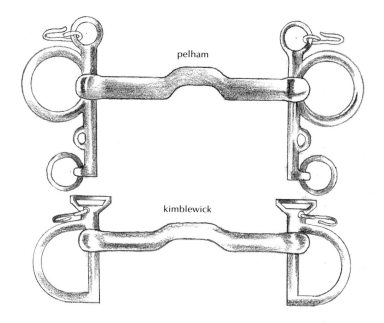

in the pony's mouth rather than direct action on the mouth as with the snaffle. This makes pelhams generally stronger than snaffles and selecting and using them should be done carefully in novice hands. When in doubt always ask advice. Many young riders on strong ponies use an ordinary pelham, often with one rein attached to a leather rounding between the snaffle and curb rings, or one rein attached to the curb ring only. Both methods are technically incorrect, but can prove advantageous. Seek advice for your own situation.

MARTINGALES

When jumping, ponies are often fitted with martingales which in general are used to prevent the pony from throwing his head beyond the point of control. They should not be used to tie the pony's head down.

Standing martingales These consist of a strap between the noseband and girth and attached to a neck strap. When fitted correctly, the martingale should reach nearly into the pony's gullet (between his jaws). When the martingale comes into

A pony correctly tacked up for jumping.

The incorrect use of draw reins, as shown here, is unfortunately a common sight. The rider is using the rein alone to force the pony's head back into an incorrect position, behind the vertical. The rider's leg has come too far back and is ineffective. Schooling devices should only ever be used for limited periods in experienced hands.

A drop noseband and a variation, the Grakle, help to prevent a horse from opening his mouth to evade the action of the bit. They should not be fitted so low that they interfere with the horse's breathing.

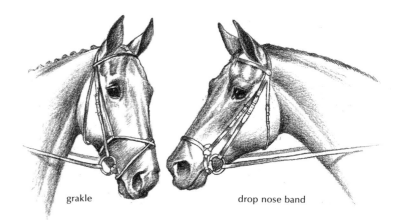

grakle   drop nose band

play there is no direct, possibly harmful, action on the horse's mouth. They should not be fitted with a drop noseband.

Running martingales Attach at one end to the girth, between the pony's legs, and divide into two straps, each with a ring at the end, through which the reins pass. When fitted correctly, the straps should reach the withers when taken together to one side. Rubber martingale stops should always be fitted between the bit and the ring.

OTHER GADGETS AND BOOTS

When attending a show-jumping competition you will undoubtedly see many horses with all types of rein and martingale attached. Often these are used indiscriminately and incorrectly, pulling the horse's nose into his chest in a most unnatural way. A horse does not approach his fences like this when loose, and should not be forced to under saddle.

Any kind of gadget which forces the horse to carry his head in an unnatural way is either incorrectly fitted or incorrectly used. In knowledgeable, sympathetic hands, such devices as draw reins or running reins may be used for a limited time in particular circumstances. They should not be used as a matter of course, nor by a novice rider unless under instruction.

Jumping puts all kinds of strains and stresses on a pony's legs and it is as well to protect them as best you can. Brushing boots should be fitted to the front legs at least, to prevent the pony

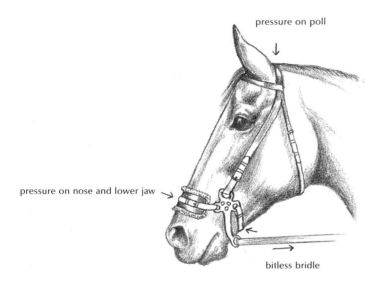

pressure on poll

pressure on nose and lower jaw

bitless bridle

Bitless bridles are sometimes used for ponies whose mouths have been ruined. They have quite a strong action, however, and should be used sensitively.

from striking one leg with the other. Overreach boots should also be fitted over the front feet to prevent the hind feet from damaging the front heels, especially in heavy going. Boots should always be kept clean and supple or they may well chafe the pony's legs.

CARE AND FITTING OF TACK

All saddlery – bridles, bits, saddles – should be adjusted correctly to fit an individual pony. At a riding school, a bridle may have been used on a different pony, so don't assume that it is adjusted correctly for the one you are about to tack up. Hold the bridle against the side of the pony's head before fitting, just to make sure it is about right. When fitted, the bit should give the pony a slight 'smile'.

Tack should be cleaned at the end of each day and numnahs washed regularly. This not only ensures that tack is kept in good condition and is comfortable for the horse, but it gives you an opportunity to spot immediately when repairs may be due.

In a perfect world we would all be wonderfully sympathetic riders with beautifully schooled horses and problems would never arise. Unfortunately, problems do arise and it is the job of trainers and experienced riders to enter the mind of the horse, or perhaps the pupil, to discover why.

THE HUMAN ELEMENT

Usually when problems arise with horses they have been man-made in the first place. A horse's education starts with the way it is handled from a foal, and that handling – or lack of it – can begin to cause problems long before formal training ever begins. In all your handling of horses, never blame the horse for his mistakes. Horses learn by memory and often the bad memories will take much time, patience and sympathetic handling to eliminate. Your own impatience and lack of understanding may make new problems or old ones worse.

Let's look at the more common jumping problems to decide why the *horse* does what he does, and how the *rider* may be corrected.

REFUSALS

There are five reasons why a horse or pony may refuse: overfacing of horse and/or rider; lack of confidence; poor riding; fear of jumping/pain; and naughtiness.

Overfacing of horse and rider Presenting a pony at a fence which is beyond his (or your) capabilities will cause problems. However bold and ambitious you feel, you should keep the height and spread of your jumps well within your ability to clear successfully.

While you are still learning you should always ride an experienced pony, but don't be tempted to overface yourself by jumping big fences. Any nervousness you have will transmit to the horse and he may stop. Alternatively, he may take the fence but you may be jumped out of the saddle in the process, resulting in a fall.

If your pony is bold, he may tackle a big jump but in doing so he may frighten or hurt himself. The memory of this will cause

him to be more cautious in the future. It takes only a moment to destroy confidence and a long time to rebuild it.

Lack of confidence   This comes as a direct result of overfacing, instilling negative associations among both horse and rider. The only way to restore confidence is to have a complete break and then return to the earliest lessons. Horse and rider should re-learn, first by stepping over single poles at the walk, then progressing gradually to trotting poles and grids. By slowly and patiently retraining, confidence should be restored.

Poor riding   If you fail to present your pony correctly at a fence you have only yourself to blame when he stops. Remember that your approach is of greatest importance. Make an accurate turn towards your fence, looking in the direction you want to go. Sit up, ride forward and straight, in balance and regular rhythm. Keep your leg *on*, working against the pony's side, until the moment he takes off. If your leg stops working, or if

Presenting a pony at a fence which is beyond his – or your – capabilities will cause problems.

Lack of confidence on the part of the rider will transmit to the horse, resulting in a refusal.

A straight approach.

your seat weakens by tipping forward, your pony may give up as well.

If you fail to stay with your pony over a fence, bending forward from the hips and allowing him freedom to stretch his head and neck forward, you will restrict his movement. This may give him a jab in the mouth from the bit as you land – another bad memory.

Pain or fear of jumping   If a pony consistently experiences pain when jumping he will soon start to refuse. Poor riding could be one cause of pain in the mouth, but there are others. Poorly fitted tack may pinch or rub, making jumping uncomfortable, and set up resistances such as head shaking, leaning on the bit, tail swishing or raising the head beyond the point of control.

Worn shoes may cause the pony to slip, and untrimmed feet will place too much strain on his legs, especially when landing. This may result in soreness and stiffness the next time he jumps and he will gradually give up any enthusiasm he had.

If a bold pony is regularly asked to tackle fences which are beyond his stage of training or physical capabilities he may be frightened into refusing to jump, or he may strain muscles in his back which may give rise to pain and long-term problems.

Always make fences inviting and introduce 'spooky' fences gradually. Don't make practice fences over 3ft (0.9m) in height. Make sure that take-offs and landings are always level and ground conditions good. Practice poles should be heavy and easily dislodged. Flimsy poles are not so well seen by a horse and he could get his legs tangled.

Naughtiness   Occasionally, if inexperienced or weak riders have allowed a pony to get away with refusals which have no cause other than mischievousness, it will be necessary to smack him once and ride him forward strongly into his fences.

RUSHING

A horse may rush towards his fences because of excitability or a lack of training, which could lead to lack of confidence. He will also rush if he anticipates pain from ill-fitting tack or bad bitting.

Ponies which tend to become excitable when jumping

Running Out
This is another form of refusal, usually caused by bad presentation. Ride straight towards your fences and do not attempt to come in at an angle. If the pony doesn't run out but attempts the fence he may give himself a fright.

Make all your fences wide, low and inviting, with a good ground line and wide wings, to help keep your pony straight into his fences. You can help keep the pony into the centre of his fences by placing poles on each side of, and at 90 degrees to, the fence on the approach. Slope the poles from the fence to the ground or have them slightly raised so that the pony finds he has to jump something. Two poles resting on the jump and arranged to make a triangle with a placing pole also help to keep the pony straight.

Running out is really a rider problem and going back a stage or two, presenting the pony in a balanced, active trot, may help the situation.

Running out is a rider problem caused by poor presentation.

should be exercised generally in a calming, relaxing way and not given too much jumping. Single jumps can be added as an extension of flat work until the pony learns to make calm, controlled approaches. Riding on a circle in front of a fence and incorporating the fence within the circle when the pony has settled is helpful. Rebalance the pony and settle him before attempting to jump again.

If the pony lacks training, return to basics and do not allow him to break into canter before the fence. Rushing away from a fence or landing out of balance are associated problems and you must be ready to sit up and rebalance your pony. Your instructor may use a pole one or two non-jumping strides after the fence to help you pick the pony up again and steady him.

REFUSING COMBINATION FENCES

This is usually a rider problem. If you allow your pony to land in a heap from the first element, you cannot expect him to make it to the second. Often novice riders lack confidence at this type of fence and fail to ride the pony forward. You must sit up, look up, and keep the pony straight, riding every inch of

the way. Horses need plenty of impulsion to negotiate combination fences and you should maintain this throughout the fence. Gridwork over small fences is your preparation for combination fences and you should gain confidence here before progressing. Ride positively.

By putting the horse on a circle instead of taking the next fence, the rider attempts to prevent him from rushing through the exercise.

TAKING OFF TOO EARLY OR TOO LATE

These are common problems. Standing off from a fence or taking off too early may be caused by rushing as a result of lack of balance, or by a very bold horse. The horse will tend to flatten or hollow over the fence, not achieving sufficient height, or he may dislodge a pole as his hind legs come down too early. Once again, returning to basics is the answer.

Jump out of trot rather than canter and use placing poles to

Do not be tempted to look down while jumping: always look where you are going.

Horses need plenty of impulsion to negotiate grids or they will run out of steam and refuse.

present the pony correctly. Gridwork and low, wide parallels help the pony to pick up his forelegs and round his back. When the pony does stretch his head and neck, you must allow with your hands to avoid causing pain in his mouth and restricting him.

When a pony gets in too close to a fence he may lack ability or confidence. Ascending rails or the use of a placing pole help him to make a better take-off. Your instructor may gradually increase the distances between fences in grids and combinations to encourage a longer stride into his fences.

UNDERSTANDING PONIES

Trying to work out what makes ponies tick is the study of a lifetime. If you can keep an understanding attitude and use common sense it will help you to remain on the right track. Try to read the signs a pony is giving you and appreciate them – don't be worried or tell him off for a squeal and a buck after the first couple of fences; he is just telling you that he enjoys life and loves his work!

Riding across country is something that you probably started early in your riding career without really thinking about it. Most riding schools combine lessons in the school with hacks in the countryside. The earliest outings can teach you much about riding over different terrain and differing ground conditions; how to maintain balance by altering your position, and how to be considerate to your pony at all times.

RIDING IN THE COUNTRYSIDE

In any kind of ride across country, even the quietest hack, you need to ride with due consideration for: fitness of your pony; level of your experience; terrain; ground conditions; and other country users.

The earliest outings can teach you much about riding over different terrain and differing ground conditions, and how to be considerate to your pony at all times.

Fitness of pony   Your pony should always be in good condition for the work you want to do. Whether stabled or at grass, he should receive the correct amount of feed for the work he does. His regular exercise will ensure that he does not sweat up unduly, nor continue to breath rapidly when you move

from a faster to a slower pace. Your riding school pony receives sufficient work to keep him fit, but your own or your friend's pony may need extra, slower work if he is ridden only once a week. If you are not sure about the fitness of a pony, or you need guidelines for getting him fit or fitter, you should seek expert advice.

Level of experience Never be tempted to ride out on a horse or pony which is beyond your ability to handle. Horses become much more excitable when outside the confines of the school or field, and you must make sure that you can handle your pony. It is tempting to want to ride different ponies but more sensible to stay with one you know. A riding school should always make sure you are not 'overhorsed'.

Terrain Different types of countryside need different styles of riding. The general rule is to stay in balance with your pony while remaining in a position which gives you the most secure seat. For uphill work you should take your weight forward on to your thighs and knees and allow your pony to pull forward with his head and neck on a long rein. Getting up off his back enables him to use his loins and quarters to push himself forward. When riding downhill your weight needs to come

Different types of countryside need different styles of riding.

When riding a drop fence your weight needs to come back to prevent the horse from falling on his forehand.

back a little behind the vertical to prevent your pony from coming down too fast and out of balance. The same rule applies when tackling drop fences, when the landing side is lower than the take-off. When the pony is travelling downhill he is more likely to stumble, or peck, on landing, but if you are positioned back you can help him pick himself up.

Ground conditions Heavy going or hard going both require considerate riding. Riding too fast on either will place great strain on your pony's legs and the old saying 'no foot no 'oss' means that if your pony is lame you have nothing to ride. If you are jumping in deep going or on hard ground the strain is even greater, and you should take things very carefully. If in doubt it is better not to jump if conditions are not reasonable. Some people fit studs to their horse's shoes in hard conditions, believing this will help the pony to hold the ground better. In fact if it is very hard, the stud will not penetrate the ground and, because of its unbalancing effect on the foot and leg, will cause even greater strain. Only fit studs on expert advice.

Stony or rocky ground should be tackled very carefully. Your pony could slip or stumble, causing injury to you both. Riding too fast over flinty ground could result in cuts from flying stones.

If you are practising in water, always make sure that your entry is as inviting as possible, with plenty of light. Avoid entering water amongst trees where the pony may have to go from bright sunlight into shadow. When riding through a stream be careful that the stream bed is safe and not slippery, nor too rocky and uneven.

Other country users   In all your riding in the countryside have consideration for, and be courteous to, other country users. Do not ride across farmland unless you have permission and keep to bridle-paths where they cross farms. Slow down for walkers and acknowledge thoughtful motorists. Do not ride on footpaths and, when the going gets deep and muddy, use common sense on whether it is wise to use bridle-paths.

CROSS-COUNTRY JUMPS

When you have shown that you can handle a pony competently on hacks, and perhaps when you have done some jumping at your riding school, natural obstacles make good practice fences. Fallen trees or branches, banks and ditches, all give you the opportunity to have a *pop*. If you are unaccompanied, do not attempt anything you're not sure of and don't tackle anything over 24–30in (60–75cm). Make sure that the take-offs and landings are good and that you have a clear line of exit away from the fence; it's not a good idea to jump 'trappy' little obstacles surrounded by trees.

If you are jumping into water, do not approach too fast. The water depth should not exceed 12in (30cm) and the landing should not be slippery nor thick with mud. The drag of the water on the pony's legs will slow him down considerably and mud adds to the problem. You should position yourself slightly back on landing to help the pony to compensate for this slowing down.

Rider's Position
For jumping cross-country fences your jumping position should be adapted to suit the task in hand. Watch three-day event riders and compare their style with a show-jumper. You will see that they bring their bodies forward only in the take-off. The position over the fence is more upright and on landing the rider keeps his body upright to help re-balance the horse. The rider's seat bones remain in contact with the saddle so that at all times he is in a position to apply the forward aids and to remain in a position of balance with the horse. On landing, especially from banks or drop fences, the rider must be ready to pick up the reins quickly again and ride forward.

Approach water and ride
through it steadily.

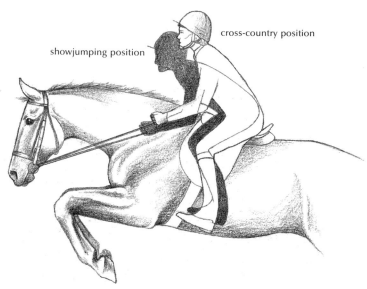

showjumping position

cross-country position

Compare the eventer's style
of riding with the show-
jumper's.

PRACTISING CROSS-COUNTRY JUMPING

Many people still get valuable cross-country jumping experience by following foxhounds or harriers. Hunts are responsible for building and maintaining hunt jumps to take the followers safely across farm hedges, fences and ditches. These are the types of fence you are likely to meet in hunter trials or events. Horses and ponies are always very excited by hunting and will jump far more fluently than in their normal environment, less bothered by 'spooky' fences or holes in the ground. Hunting gives ponies an added enthusiasm for jumping which is carried on into their show-jumping or competitive cross-country.

You must be sure that you are suitably mounted for hunting, as three or four hours on a strong pony could spoil your day and destroy your confidence. Most hunts have special meets once or twice a season for Pony Club members, which is a good introduction. If you don't want to follow foxhounds, you can follow an aniseed trail or the track of a runner with draghounds or bloodhounds. The mounted followers will ride a set line with many fences and you should really be fairly experienced to take part here, as they travel fast and the fences are often big.

A gentler introduction to a course of cross-country fences may be a sponsored ride when you might be able to ride as a

There is no minimum age limit for hunting! Most hunts have special children's and Pony Club meets during the season which runs from November to April.

pair with a friend. This is especially helpful as an introduction to give you added confidence and also to give you a lead over fences of which you may be unsure. When you are learning it is much easier to ride positively on a pony going forward than one which is backing off all the way into a fence.

HOW TO RIDE CROSS-COUNTRY FENCES

The more experienced you get, the bigger the fences you will tackle. The rules for riding cross country remain the same, however. All cross-country fences should be treated with respect, no matter how small or straightforward they appear to be. Most of them will be fixed and cannot be knocked down; if you pony knocks one he will probably bruise himself at the least, and at the worst, fall, taking you with him. Your intro-

Confidence is essential for cross-country jumping.

duction to cross-country fences should be on a safe, experienced pony who will take care of you and keep you out of trouble. You will then gain confidence in jumping over this type of fence, which is essential for cross-country riding.

TYPES OF FENCE

All cross-country fences need bold, accurate riding, but some types of fence will need stronger riding and a very confident approach by pony and rider. The general categories, which are adorned in different ways by course builders, are: ditches and open water; uprights; spreads; banks; steps and drop fences; water; combinations; corners and coffins.

Ditches and open water These may cause the pony to look twice before jumping, but you must encourage him to jump the obstacle without looking; the first rule for the rider is not to be tempted to look yourself! Look straight ahead and forget about the ditch. Sometimes ditches are dressed with a single, raised rail across the top (a trakehner) or rails arranged as a pyramid over the ditch (a tiger trap). These sorts of fences need to be ridden boldly, but often their appearance frightens the rider more than they do the pony!

Upright fences Jumping these fences is usually straightforward, unless the ground line is indistinct and the pony gets in too close. If the fence comes after a canter uphill, you should ask the pony to come back to an energetic, bouncy stride to make sure his hocks are underneath him. If you are riding downhill towards an upright you should steady and rebalance your pony to get him back onto his hocks before the take-off.

Banks These are built in some parts of the country as field boundaries and a pony will briefly land on the top, pushing off again with his hind legs. Always ride straight at a bank and keep riding forward with energy, from take-off to landing.

Steps and drop fences If you have to ride up steps you must keep the pony bouncing upwards, which needs plenty of energy in reserve. *Steps down* or *drop fences* should be

Water
This should be approached steadily but with plenty of impulsion to compensate for the drag on the pony's legs when landing. Open water should be approached in gallop, when the pony will take it in his stride.

Spreads
The rider should approach a spread with his pony balanced and with plenty of energy in hand, but not too slowly. The take-off should be not too far off (which would make the spread wider), nor too close (which may cause the pony to knock his legs on the first rail). You should allow your pony to stretch his head and neck over the fence.

stile

zig-zag

tiger trap and ditch

bank

trakehner

corner

approached steadily in trot. You should position yourself back to prevent the pony from falling on his nose on landing, and be ready to pick him up again and ride forward.

Combinations As with show jumps, combinations comprise two or three parts with a varying number of strides between each element. For novices these will be straightforward and the striding should be easy for the majority of ponies in the class. You should remember your gridwork and ride for a point beyond the last element. Keep pushing the pony forward positively and keep him straight. As you gain experience, you may attempt jumping the 'corner' of a 'V'-fence. This should be ridden very accurately, so that you do not ride too close to the flag so as to risk a run out, nor too far into the fence giving too wide a spread.

Coffins You are likely only to meet this type of fence when you are much more experienced. Coffins are usually ditches approached by an upright, a downhill slope and followed by a slope to another upright. The pony should be kept steady and in balance, and the rider should be experienced and agile enough to keep with the movement at all times.

Competitions are tremendously exciting and your first show ever will have you on a knife-edge of thrills and trepidation. Careful planning, preparation and knowledge of your pony's and your own abilities and limitations are the keys to an enjoyable outing.

PREPARATION FOR THE FIRST SHOW

If you are borrowing a riding school pony, he will be familiar with being with other horses, but not strange horses or surroundings. Your own pony may not be used to seeing lots of other horses and this could be so exciting for him that he forgets all about those hours of careful schooling at home. If possible, before actually competing, take your pony to one or two outings just to allow him to grow familiar with the show atmosphere.

At whatever level you aim, you will still need instruction and you should not neglect the all-important flat work or dressage. A show-jumping round should be ridden fluently, not in fits and starts, and that can only be achieved by correct schooling. Your jumping schooling should consist of athletic grids, nothing more than 3ft (0.9m) high – practising over puissance fences won't make you a good show-jumper.

MAKING YOUR ENTRY

At most novice shows, entries can be made on the day if classes are not full, but you will undoubtedly feel happier if this is done beforehand. Read the schedule and the rules carefully and make sure you have filled in the entry form correctly. A parent (if you are not old enough) may need to sign the form and will also probably need to give you a cheque for the entry fee. Note the closing date for entries and post yours off in good time. Late entries are usually accepted, but cost more.

Ask your instructor's advice and don't be over-ambitious for your first outing; two classes should be enough. On the day, a couple of rounds in the clear-round jumping will help to give you confidence and familiarize your pony with the surroundings. Don't overface yourselves; enter for classes which you

Planning the Day
When planning the day itself, work backwards from the time of the start of the first class for which you have entered, asking yourself:

How long will I need to work in and do clear rounds?
How long will it take to tack up and unload?
How long to find the secretary, toilets, etc?
How long to reach the show ground?
How long to load my pony if he sometimes proves difficult?
How long to groom, plait (if necessary) and prepare for travelling?
How long for my pony to eat his morning feed and for me to have breakfast?

Once you have answered all these questions, you will know for when to set your alarm clock!

A show-jumping round should be ridden fluently, not in fits and starts.

Enter for classes which you feel are easily within your capabilities.

A young rider neatly turned out for a show-jumping competition. For extra protection the pony could be wearing overreach and brushing boots.

feel are easily within your capabilities, rather than stretching them.

GETTING READY

A good deal of preparation can be done the day before. All the tack should be clean and put ready, along with sweat sheet/cooler, buckets, water and hay net for the return journey, and possibly small feed for the competition. All your own clothes – show or hacking jacket, shirt and tie, jodhpurs and clean boots, jockey skull and silk (black or navy), stick – could be loaded in the car. It is best to wear old clothes until you get to the show and then change. Make a picnic if you think you'll be able to eat.

In the morning, don't forget you will also need to load your grooming kit into the car, once you have finished your initial preparations. Many people don't worry about plaiting for small competitions but it would give you practice and it does show that you have taken the time and trouble to be neatly turned out.

WORKING IN AT THE SHOW

You should have given yourself plenty of time before the start of your class, barring punctures and breakdowns. Unless your pony is crashing about in the trailer or lorry, desperate to get out, leave him where he is while you collect your number and find out which ring you will be in, and where it is. On no account leave your pony tied up unattended outside the trailer; even inside he could get into difficulty if left. Best of all, unload him and ask a parent or friend to walk him round quietly.

On returning, get yourself ready, then your pony, and get straight on. Check your stirrups and girth and, reassuring your pony with one or two good pats, make your way to the practice area. If he is disturbed by others cantering and jumping past him, try to find somewhere a little away from the others to begin with and gradually move closer.

There are no hard and fast rules for how long you should ride before you enter the arena because this will depend on the pony and you should know your pony. Don't neglect the flat work and when you want to jump, just make two or three good attempts over perhaps a small spread or parallel and leave it at that. Before the start of the class give the steward your number and he will write this on a board which will then be the order of riding. When the course is ready the competitors are invited to walk it.

WALKING THE COURSE

For the first few shows, don't get too bogged down with too many technicalities. The course should have been well built to cater for an approximate height of pony, so don't panic about striding out between fences. By all means, when you practise or if you have time to think about it at the show, count your actual strides into a fence and between the elements of a combination, but don't ride for a stride. The most important consideration when walking the course is to plan your track; where you will turn in order to approach your fences straight and in balance. Then just concentrate on riding your pony forward and straight around your planned track. This is when your flat work will pay off.

Remember that you may need to ride more strongly past the collecting ring or horse box park, as your pony may tend to hang towards these, and you could prepare for this by carrying your stick on that side, to reinforce your leg aid. If you are riding in an indoor jumping competition, remember that distances tend to be shorter and turns tighter than outdoors. Keep an eye on those going into the ring and perhaps watch some good riders to see how they ride the course. Be nearby when it is nearing your turn so that you don't hold up proceedings, and be ready to enter the ring when the steward asks.

If you should ride well enough to go clear, you must decide whether you are ready to cope with a jump off. There will be plenty more shows at which to win rosettes, yet it could take a long time to restore confidence if you overface yourself. If things go wrong, if your pony refuses or knocks his fences, accept this in good grace and philosophically. Do not try to teach your pony a lesson in the ring; accept that quite probably the error is yours. Jumping faults accumulate at four for each fence down, three for each refusal up to a total of three refusals, which result in elimination. Decide to concentrate on particular problems at home.

MANAGING YOUR PONY AT THE SHOW

It depends on how long you have between classes as to what you do in the meantime. If you have an hour or more, untack your pony, give him a drink and allow him to pick the grass for a few minutes and relax. When you finish the day it is equally important to allow your pony to relax before loading him and travelling home. The whole outing will have been quite stressful to your pony, and rushing him home could result in digestive disturbances; similarly, he should be allowed time on arrival at the show. Once again, perhaps a parent or friend would walk him round to allow him to cool down naturally and let his muscles relax while you go to thank the secretary for the day. Horse-show secretaries rarely receive the thanks they deserve and your consideration would be much appreciated.

Bandage up your pony's legs and rug him up according to the prevailing weather conditions. On arriving back at the yard, put your pony's needs before your own. If he has broken out in sweat you will need to walk him around a little before

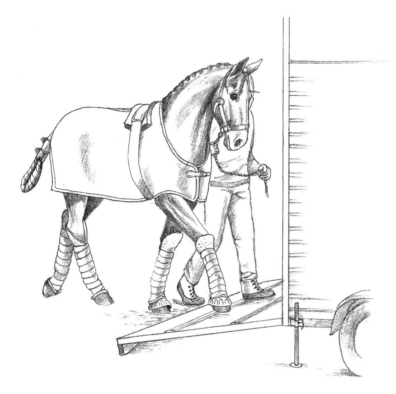

Allow plenty of time for preparation and travelling. It is not good for a pony to be rushed on arrival. This pony is correctly prepared for travelling with well-padded bandages all round, the tail bandaged and guarded and a day rug secured with a roller. When loading, always walk at the pony's shoulder and look straight ahead into the trailer.

putting on a sweat sheet underneath a summer sheet to help him dry without chilling. Your pony should have plenty of fresh water, a large hay net and, if he is to be rested next day, a bran mash as his last feed. He should be checked again through the evening to see that he hasn't broken out in sweat or isn't otherwise sick or sorry.

As for you, before you go home, muck out the trailer or lorry, clean the tack and then maybe you've earned yourself a nice hot bath!

AFTER THE SHOW

Next day the pony should be checked for soundness, then turned out in his field or paddock. If you had any problems with particular fences at the show, try to recreate them at your riding school or at home and sort the problems out once you return to work.

When you have had some experience of cross-country fences – hacking, hunting or just practising – an outing to a hunter trial helps to broaden your equestrian horizons.

Enter a hunter or eventer trial which has a reputation for well-built fences and choose a class in which the fences are lower and simpler than those you practise over at your riding school or at home. In all competitive work you should be more advanced in your work at home, so the competition is easily within your capabilities. Riding in strange surroundings always places greater demands on horse and rider without the addition of more testing obstacles.

PREPARING THE PONY

Your pony must be fit enough for the competition and you should gradually build up your pony's stamina by increasing periods of trot and canter. Getting horses and ponies fitter requires experienced help as a balance between feeding and work has to be found to suit individual requirements.

At the competition your pony will need extra attention, especially after the class, when he will be hot and sweaty. As well as a normal grooming kit, you should take a container of water, buckets, sponges and a sweat scraper, so that you can wash the pony down after his class.

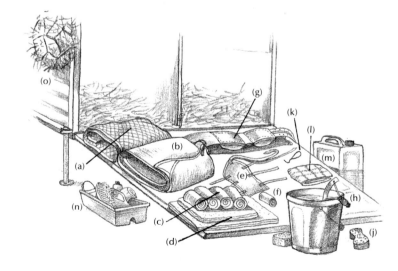

The equipment you will need to care for your pony after the competition: (a) an anti-sweat sheet; (b) a day rug; (c) stable bandages; (d) gamgee tissue; (e) a tail guard; (f) a tail bandage; (g) a roller; (h) a sweat scraper; (i) buckets; (j) sponge(s); (k) a hoof pick; (l) a towel; (m) a water container; (n) a normal grooming kit; (o) hay net.

A young rider wearing correct attire for a hunter trial.

TACK FOR YOUR PONY

You may need to use a slightly stronger bit than you usually ride with when riding across country, as some ponies tend to take a hold when excited by the situation. You may also find a martingale useful if the pony tends to hold his head high, and you can grab the neck strap if you feel yourself being left behind over a fence. All your tack should be checked for wear and tear, especially reins, girth and girth straps, and stirrup leathers. It is a good idea to fit a surcingle right around the saddle for added security. Fit brushing boots to the front legs at least and overreach boots to the front feet.

WALKING THE COURSE

Hunter trial courses are usually available to walk the day before the competition, and it saves time on the day of the event if you have already done this. If you are unsure of any particular fence you can return and look at it again before riding the course.

At novice level the fences will be straightforward and the purpose of walking the course will be to familiarize yourself with it and decide how and where to ride each fence. It is a

What to Wear
The correct wear at a hunter trial is what is known as *ratcatcher*: hacking jacket, shirt and tie, jodhpurs, riding boots and jockey skull with black or blue silk. For an eventer trial, a coloured cross-country jumper may be worn, and a silk to match. Remember that a hat is only any good if it is still on your head when you hit the ground. The chin strap should be fastened at all times.

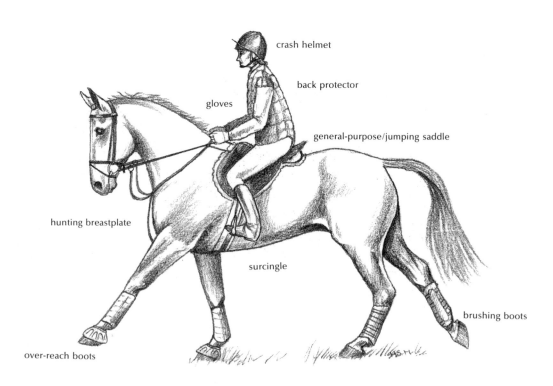

crash helmet

back protector

gloves

general-purpose/jumping saddle

hunting breastplate

surcingle

brushing boots

over-reach boots

A pony correctly tacked up for a cross-country competition.

good idea to take your instructor or an experienced rider with you to give advice. The fences will be marked by flags, red to the right and white to the left, and you should make sure that you do not jump outside these markers. If a time-saving alternative is offered you would probably be better to take the longer, simpler route until you are confident enough of your own and your pony's ability to take the trickier route. When approaching fences at speed you need to know exactly where you plan to jump, so that you can be positive in your approach.

All your fences should be ridden boldly but with respect. Discuss with your instructor how each fence should be approached and ridden through. Note whether fences are placed downhill or uphill and what the ground is like on the take-off and landing. If you see fences which may seem a little scary, pick a distant landmark on which you can fix your eye when riding. Don't be tempted to look into the fence itself.

Look to see how well the fences are built. Sometimes in smaller competitions the fences have been less well – and sometimes badly – built. Although well-built fences con-

structed of large timbers look bigger, they actually cause far fewer problems than flimsier, less solid obstacles. Look for 'inviting' fences – those which look as though they are asking you to jump them.

You should also take into consideration the ground conditions. Soft or hard conditions will place different, and perhaps extra, stress on your pony's legs, and determine the speed at which you should travel.

You should know exactly how you plan to ride each fence in order to ride fluently and save time.

COMPETITION DAY

Your pony should have an early feed on the day of the competition, and no hay in the morning. He cannot canter across country on a stomach full of hay. Allow yourself plenty of time to prepare your pony for travel, to get to the competition in time to walk the course if necessary, and to warm him up (*see* page 76). Set times of riding are usually given and you normally get these by post or on the phone before the day of the competition.

There is no need to plait the pony's mane, but tails may be plaited and tied up if the going is very muddy. Check all your tack and equipment and have your own clothes ready to change into once all your work around the pony is finished.

On arrival at the competition, check that your pony has not suffered any injuries during the journey, or been sweating up in excitement. In any case, it might be a good idea to unload him and ask a friend or parent to walk him round while you go to collect your number from the secretary. If there is time – and you should have built time into your day's timetable – walk the course quickly again or at least return to any fences of which you may be unsure.

Your pony will need to have a warm-up to make sure his muscles are nicely loosened and working efficiently before you ask him to canter and jump. Get on your pony 15–30 minutes before your time, and spend a few minutes just walking quietly around, familiarizing yourselves with the competition atmosphere. Build up to trot and canter, then have two or three jumps over the practice fence. Keep your pony on the move but don't spend all the time galloping and jumping; he will need as much energy as possible for the course.

Be near the start as your time approaches to avoid holding anyone up. Check your girth and tighten it if necessary. When you are told to go, set off at a steady canter. Remember that you have to complete the course and if you tear off at the beginning you may not make it to the end. Be especially careful of uphill stretches, which will exhaust your pony if you go too fast.

If your pony refuses at a fence, you have two more chances at it. Three refusals mean elimination and the judge at the fence will let you know. Sometimes at novice competitions you are allowed to complete the course as a practice, but you are out of the competition. If this is the case, be careful that you do not obstruct the other competitors. Get out of the way of people coming up quickly from behind.

Pairs Classes
Often a hunter trial has a pairs class where two riders complete the course together. If you are unsure of yourself, or nervous about competitions, it helps to feel you are not alone. The more experienced rider can go ahead and act as a lead. If you are ever introducing a young pony to competitions, a pairs class can help to give the pony confidence.

AFTER YOUR ROUND

Your pony will need to warm down after his round to relax his muscles again, and the walk back to your trailer should help. Don't let him stand and get chilled. If he has sweated up, wash him off with water and a sponge and remove the excess water

with a sweat scraper. Fit an anti-sweat sheet, or cooler, securing it with a roller, and walk your pony round. He should soon stop breathing hard from his exertion and, as he cools, place a day rug or summer sheet over the sweat-sheet, folding the front corners back under the roller. This will help to keep him warm. Offer him a drink once he has stopped blowing, but try to prevent the water from getting too cold.

If your pony's legs and tail are muddy, wash these off as well and check for injuries or any thorns he may have picked up. If you are worried about anything there should be a vet available at the competition to help you. Bandage your pony's legs and prepare him for the journey home. If the journey is quite long, give him a hay net in the trailer to help him settle.

Your pony must be fit enough for the competition. Ride considerately and be careful of uphill stretches which can really take it out of your pony if you go too fast. Take note also of the ground conditions: soft ground will be especially tiring while hard ground may jar your pony's legs.

HOME AGAIN

If you have borrowed a pony from your riding school, don't just hand him over and go home. Take him to his box, unbandage his legs, and ask advice on whether it is necessary to wash them again. A quick brush with a body brush may be all that is necessary. Make sure the pony is comfortable and not showing any signs of distress, nor beginning to sweat again. A good, warm bran mash should be prepared for him to which you could add some sliced carrots as his reward. After a cross-country competition or hunting, a pony should be checked again during the evening and last thing at night to see that he is not sweating and that everything seems to be normal. The next day he should be trotted up to check that he is sound. If all is well, he should be given the day off, preferably out in his field to allow him the chance to relax completely.

For those who wish to further their riding, the possibilities are endless. It is true to say that the more you learn the more you realize there is to learn and that, in fact, you will never know it all. Rather than putting you off, this becomes part of the fascination – every horse provides a different challenge and teaches you something new.

Naturally, anyone who learns to ride has dreams of one day owning their own pony or horse. Although ownership may mean more opportunities to practise, it does not necessarily help you to improve your riding. In fact, it may prevent you from progressing if you discontinue regular lessons. Rather than entering too quickly into ownership, money may be better spent on frequent lessons and concentrated courses during the holidays. Your own riding school will probably offer these, but it can be greater fun to have a riding holiday away from home when you will have the opportunity to ride different horses. Sometimes progress seems slow when you can ride

Even if you have your own pony, continue to have regular lessons.

only one hour a week, so a week's course when you may ride two to four hours a day can really give you a boost. Sometimes something you have been unable to do or understand with your regular instructor suddenly becomes clear when taught in a slightly different way by someone new.

During all the school holidays, your local Pony Club branch will hold regular instructional rallies and these full days are a further opportunity to improve. You need not own a pony to join the Pony Club and unmounted as well as mounted rallies are organized. Your riding school will probably have links with the Pony Club and will be pleased to let you hire a pony for mounted rallies. The Pony Club offers a series of tests, graded according to age and ability, starting with the 'D' test and reaching a very high standard at 'A' test. These combine testing your riding with your horse and stable management knowledge, which is obviously essential if you plan to own a pony.

Through the Pony Club or riding club you will gain an introduction to the various competitive sports – eventing, show-jumping, dressage, long-distance riding – and there is an opportunity for everyone to take part at whatever level. Taking

The Pony Club will give you an introduction to the competitive sports. An athletic helper is needed for leading rein show-jumping.

Make sure you prepare adequately for whatever you want to do. A competitor in a show class gives her individual show.

part in competitions is always nerve-racking when you start and even when you get more experienced, but don't be put off because you think you may not be good enough. There is only one way to find out. What you should always do is make sure you have prepared adequately for whatever you want to do. Visiting some shows unmounted to see how the various competitions are run and what you will be expected to do will help familiarize yourself with the show scene. Never be afraid to ask for advice from an instructor or experienced competitor and practise thoroughly. Check on what to wear, what tack may be used on the pony and make sure your arrive in plenty of time to get organized once at the show. Competitive riding may seem a big step forward, but stretching yourself towards goals helps you to progress more quickly through the practical experience it gives you.

WHICH EVENT?

If you are interested in cross-country riding, the best starter would be to take part in a minimus with 20–28in (50–70cm) jumps, or a novice hunter trial with jumps under 3ft 3in (1m). Similar events are held for show-jumping, while dressage tests start at preliminary level and consist of no more than the basic school movements you are used to already. The Pony Club has its own dressage tests and riding clubs have what is known as Prix Caprilli, which combines basic school exercises with negotiating a small jump. This is judged purely on the perform-

If you are interested in cross country, start with a minimus class.

The preliminary dressage tests consist of no more than basic school exercises with which you are familiar.

ance of the rider, rather than horse and rider, so is a good assessment of your progressing skills. Combining your flat work with jumping prepares you for horse trials, where the competition consists of show-jumping, dressage and cross country.

BUYING A PONY

If you get to the stage of buying a pony, do first make sure you have the time, facilities and resources to look after him properly. Do not be tempted to buy either the first one you see, or a pony beyond your own ability. Young horses in the early stages of their education are cheaper to buy than a similar animal which is well schooled, but the training of horses is for experienced people only and you should be very careful about taking on such a challenge. Always seek professional and veterinary advice and do continue to have lessons.

Whether or not you have a pony of your own, don't forget to have a lesson on the lunge occasionally to correct faults which may creep in. When you find a good instructor, stay with her, rather than flit from person to person as this will confuse you rather than teach. An occasional visit to another teacher or attending a visiting teacher's clinic can be helpful sometimes to throw new light on a problem. The opportunity occasionally to ride a more highly schooled horse than you are used to will also help you to get the feel of movements correctly performed which will help you to improve your own performance.

Improving Your Skills
As you become increasingly involved in any sport, your riding skills should be matched by your knowledge and ability to train and prepare the pony for the job you want him to do. The more demanding sports involving jumping mean that the horse has to get progressively and specifically fitter over a period which may range from weeks at the beginner stage to months or even years of preparation at the most advanced stages. Becoming interested at the early stages in horse management is an essential part of progressing in these sports.

Canter lead   The leading leg in canter is the leg which steps forward last in a canter stride. When cantering on the right rein the right foreleg usually leads; on the left rein the left foreleg will lead. Canter is three-time; there are three steps to a stride. In canter on the right rein, the left hindleg steps forward first, followed by the right hindleg and left foreleg together, and the stride is completed by the right foreleg. (Left canter starts on the right hindleg and finishes on the left foreleg).

Change the rein   Change direction, from the right to the left rein, or vice versa. This can be done in several ways, the most common are:
1. *Across the diagonal*   Between K–M or F–H, passing through X.
2. *Across the centre of the school*   E–X–B or B–X–E.
3. *Down the centre line*   A–X–C or C–X–A.

Combination fences   Two or three jumps built in a line and at distances related to one another form the elements of a double or treble combination fence. The elements are all part of the same fence, numbered parts A, B and C. In competition, refusal at the second or third parts means the whole combination must be jumped again.

Dressage test   A given sequence of between twelve to twenty school movements to be performed accurately, in order, by horse and rider. The level of test ranges from simple riding school movements in walk, trot and canter to the international Grand Prix level where highly trained horses and riders include movements such as piaffe and passage and one-time canter changes. Dressage arenas measure 20m × 40m or 20m × 60m.
Marks are awarded out of ten for each movement, the winner being the rider with the highest score. In eventing the dressage score is converted to penalty points, so that the lowest score is best.

'Flat' work   Work done in the school excluding jumping.

Ground line   A line defined usually by a pole on the ground, or the baseline of a solid fence, which enables horse and rider to assess the take-off point for a fence.

Half-halt   A momentary collection of the horse, used to gain his attention in preparation for transitions, changes of direction, and jumping. The half-halt helps to bring the horse back on to his hocks and move forward correctly. Sit tall and deep, pushing the horse up into a restraining hand, as though to halt, but soften the hand and send him on again immediately once he has responded.

High school or 'haute ècole'   Movements include piaffe, passage and the elevated 'airs above the ground' made famous by the Spanish Riding School of Vienna.

Impulsion   The energy created in the horse's quarters to propel him forward into action

Independent seat   The rider's ability to maintain balance and control of his own body and actions, so that he does not interfere with the horse.

Inside rein The one which corresponds with the inner bend of the horse, usually nearer the centre of the school.

Jumping track The path horse and rider travel around a whole course of jumps, including approaches, take-offs and landings.

Lengthened strides The pony lengthens his stride in any gait when his hind legs step a little further underneath him and his forelegs correspondingly reach further forward, with no loss of rhythm. The lenthening must come from the quarters, as the more active 'engaged' hocks send the pony forward.

Nearside The left side of the horse.

Offside The right side of the horse.
On the left rein Going anti-clockwise around the school.
On the right rein Going clockwise around the school.
Outside rein Whichever rein you are on, the one which corresponds with the outside bend of the horse (nearer the outside of the school usually).

Pace Also known as gait. Walk, trot, canter and gallop are the horse's different paces.

Rhythm Regularity of hoofbeats within a gait.

Stride The horse completes a stride when all four feet have stepped forward.

Track right (or left) On reaching the track, go to the right (or left).
Transition Moving from one pace to another.
Trot diagonal In rising trot you should sit when the horse's outside shoulder comes back towards you. If you are on the wrong diagonal, sit for one extra stride.

Xenophon A Greek soldier of the third century BC whose writings, which were translated into the *Art of Horsemanship*, are a classic amongst equestrian literature.

3-loop serpentine A double 'S' starting at A or C.
20-metre circle This usually means a circle covering half of the school you are in, touching the track at C or A and passing through X. A circle is a continual turn and the horse should not dwell on the track. A circle in the centre of the school starts at E or B with X as the centre.

British Horse Society
British Equestrian Centre
Stoneleigh
Kenilworth
Warwickshire CV8 2LR

Association of British Riding Schools
Old Brewery Yard
Penzance
Cornwall TR18 2SL

British Show Hack, Cob and Riding Horse
  Association
Rookwood
Packington Park
Meriden
Warwickshire CV7 7HG

British Show Jumping Association
British Equestrian Centre
Stoneleigh
Kenilworth
Warwickshire CV8 2LR

Farriers Registration Council
PO Box 49
East of England Showground
Peterborough
Cambridgeshire PE2 0GU

Horses and Ponies Protection Association
64 Station Road
Padiham
Lancashire BB12 8EF

Hunters Improvement and National Light
  Horse Breeding Society
96 High Street
Edenbridge
Kent

National Pony Society
Brook House
25 High Street
Alton
Hampshire GU34 1AW

Ponies Association of UK
Chesham House
Green End Road
Sawtry
Huntingdon
Cambridgeshire PE17 5UY

Riding for the Disabled Association
Avenue R
National Agricultural Centre
Stoneleigh
Kenilworth
Warwickshire CV8 2LY

American Farriers Association
4089 Iron Works Pike
Lexington
KY 40511

American Grandprix Association
PO Box 495
Wayne
PA 19087

American Horse Council
1700 K St., NW
Suite 300
Washington DC 20006

American Horse Protection Association
1000 29th St., NW #T–100
Washington DC 20007

American Horse Shows Association
220 E 42nd Street
Suite 409
New York
NY 10017

North American Riding for the
  Handicapped Association
PO Box 33150
Denver
CO 80233

United States Combined Training
  Association
292 Bridge Street
South Hamilton
MA 01982

United States Dressage Federation
PO Box 80668
Lincoln
NE 68501

United States Pony Clubs
893 Matlock St., #110
West Chester
PA 19382

FURTHER READING

The Pony Club Manual of Horsemanship (Pony Club, 1950)
Drummond, M   *The Horse Care and Stable Manual* (The Crowood Press, 1988)
Foster, C   *The Athletic Horse* (The Crowood Press, 1986)
Harris, C   *Fundamentals of Riding* (Association of British Riding Schools Manual, J A Allen & Co, 1985
Houghton-Brown, J and Powell-Smith, V   *Horse and Stable Management* (Blackwell Science Publications, 1987)
Mairinger, F   *Horses are Made to be Horses* (Rigby Publishers, 1983)
Podhajsky, A   *The White Stallions of Vienna* (Sportsman's Press,1985)
Rose, M   *The Horsemaster's Notebook* (Threshold Books, 1988)
Swift, S   *Centred Riding* (Heinemann, 1986)